Convicted

&

Transformed

The Christian's Relationship to the Holy Spirit

Convicted
&
Transformed

The Christian's Relationship to the Holy Spirit

Myron S. Augsburger

Foreword by Leighton Ford
Preface by Ralph I. Tilley

LITS Books
PO Box 405
Sellersburg, Indiana 47172

Convicted & Transformed:
The Christian's Relationship to the Holy Spirit

Original edition published under the title:
Quench Not the Spirit
and reprinted by arrangement with
Herald Press, Harrisonburg, Virginia 22802.
©1975 by Herald Press. All Rights Reserved.

ISBN: 10: 0990395057
ISBN: 13: 978-0-9903950-5-8

LITS Books
PO Box 405
Sellersburg, Indiana 47172

LITS Books is a division of Life in the Spirit Ministries, a 501 (c) (3) not-for-profit ministry. Donations are welcome.

Bulk discounts are available; contact editor@litsjournal.org.

This book is available on Kindle and other devices.

For all books authored or edited by Ralph I. Tilley, go to litsjournal.org or amazon.com.

To our children,
with the prayer that their lives be
filled with His Spirit

Contents

Foreword

BIBLICAL ... WARM ... BALANCED ... life-oriented ... challenging. My reaction to this book by my good friend, Myron Augsburger, could be summed up in those five words. Let me elaborate.

Much of the current discussion about the work of the Holy Spirit degenerates into a heated exchange of divergent theological viewpoints with conflicting appeals to history and experience. The Christian certainly cannot lightly dismiss the testimonies of saints either of the past or the present. Dr. Augsburger's discussion of the subject, however, brings us back to the Bible, which is the tribunal by which we test all religious experience.

But this is not a dry-as-dust, lifeless book of dogma. Too often our discussions of the work of the Holy Spirit have been clear as crystal and as cold as ice. The result has been an evangelical orthodoxy that could be described as "a giant in bonds." Dr. Augsburger's volume throbs with vitality and is characterized by a warmth that is contagious.

There is balance here that rises above a mere partisan repetition of a rigid theological stance. Like anyone else, Dr. Augsburger approaches the Scriptures with a certain viewpoint, but I detect here a fairness and balance that are remarkable. That balance comes through because the author has not felt obliged to advance some point of doctrine merely because it is a necessary part of a preconceived system.

You won't read this volume and close it with a resigned, "So what?" It is life-related—dealing with life here and now. And, after all, we derive little help or guidance from a recitation of facts about the Person and work of the Holy Spirit if the discussion is restricted to His ministry nineteen centuries ago. I sense here that what the author is saying is very much related to my experience. He meets me where I live.

The reader should feel challenged, as he puts down this book, to determine if he is enjoying in his own experience that ministry of the Holy Spirit of which the Bible speaks so clearly.

May the great Head of the Church be pleased to pour out in a fuller measure His Spirit in these days of unprecedented opportunity for Spirit-anointed churches and believers! And may He bless this in its mission of acquainting believers in Jesus Christ with the inheritance.

Leighton Ford
Charlotte, North Carolina
October 11, 1974

Preface

IT WAS MANY YEARS AGO when I first "stumbled" across a book penned by Myron S. Augsburger. Though our roots are in different church traditions, I soon discovered through his writings that here was a man who believed in "the faith that was once for all delivered to the saints" Jude 1:3), was a convinced Evangelical, exuded a contagious love for the Lord Jesus Christ, and honored the Holy Spirit throughout his writings.

One cannot read after Augsburger long before realizing that he is a man of God, possessed of a keen mind and a warm heart. By means of both his formal education obtained in the classroom, and his Christ-shaped heart and conscience formed by Word and Spirit, Augsburger has written with penetrating insight, informed conviction, and spiritual wisdom and understanding.

In addition to ministering effectively in his own Anabaptist tradition, God has given to Dr. Augsburger a wider ministry to much of the church. The Lord expanded his fellowship years ago to embrace all who call Jesus Lord and walk in fellowship with Him. This willingness to fellowship and serve alongside other Evangelicals is evidenced by the fact that Billy Graham (a Baptist) wrote the Foreword to one of his books, and Leighton Ford (son-in-law to Billy Graham and a Presbyterian) wrote the Foreword to this volume.

Some Christians write because they desire to be published. Other write because they think they can earn money. A few men and women of God write because they have something pertinent to say to the church. Dr. Augsburger falls into the latter category: he has something to say about the Holy Spirit that the church needs to hear.

While *Convicted & Transformed* (originally titled, *Quench Not the Spirit*) was first published over fifty years ago, it remains a relevant and vibrant voice to all who will listen. In many respects, the Holy Spirit is the ignored member of the Triune God in the contemporary church. Furthermore, in places where the Spirit is not ignored, His person and ministries are often misunderstood, resulting in much error and confusion.

The reader who is eager to learn about the Christian's relationship to the Holy Spirit will discover in this volume a biblically sound approach, as well as a challenge to one's conscience. *Convicted & Transformed* cannot be seriously read without often stopping to lift the heart to God, seeking His understanding and grace.

The Christian world is both blessed and indebted to those men and women of faith, who stimulate us to sink our roots deeper into the truth and wisdom of God. I thank God for giving Myron S. Augsburger to Christ's church, and I think you will too after reading this book about the Christian's relationship to the Third Person of the Holy Trinity.

Ralph I. Tilley
Soli Deo Gloria

About
Myron S. Augsburger

MYRON S. AUGSBURGER was born August 20, 1929, in Elida, Ohio, and raised in the Anabaptist tradition. He and his wife Esther have three children.

Dr. Augsburger received his Junior College Bible Diploma from Eastern Mennonite College (now University) after which he pastored the Tuttle Avenue Mennonite Church in Sarasota, Florida. He returned to Harrisonburg, Virginia in 1953 to continue his studies and serve as a part-time campus pastor at Eastern Mennonite College. He received his A.B. and Th.B. degrees from EMC. Later, he received a B.D. degree from Goshen Biblical Seminary, in Goshen, Indiana. He received his Th.M. and Th.D. from Union Theological Seminary of Virginia, while serving as a pastor at National Heights Mennonite Church. Dr. Augsburger continued his education in postgraduate studies at George Washington University; University of Michigan; University of Basel; Mansfield College; and Oxford University. He also served as a scholar in residence at Princeton Seminary. He has been awarded ten honorary doctorates.

Dr. Augsburger was the fifth president of what was then Eastern Mennonite College & Seminary, serving from 1965 to 1980. He was also professor of theology from 1963-1980.

Before going to EMU, Augsburger was a well-known evangelist who held crusades throughout the United States and Canada under the auspices of InterChurch Evangelism. He was listed in a 1969 issue of Time magazine as one of the emerging young Evangelical leaders in the U.S. Augsburger is also the author of more than 20 books, and served a term as moderator of the Mennonite Church General Assembly.

After leaving the EMU presidency, Augsburger and his wife Esther moved to Washington, D.C., where he served as president of the Council of Christian Colleges & Universities. The couple also founded a church on Capitol Hill—Washington Community Fellowship. Later, they retired to Harrisonburg, Virginia.

In September 1987, the Augsburgers spent a semester at Union Biblical Seminary in Pune, India. During their time there, Myron taught courses and Esther (a renowned artist) built a nine-foot sculpture of Jesus washing Peter's feet. At this time, he also began his work as Moderator of the General Assembly of the Mennonite Church, USA, which he held for two years.

The following is a selection of the books authored by Dr. Augsburger: *Called to Maturity, Faith for a Secular World, Walking in the Resurrection, Practicing the Presence of the Spirit, The Preacher's Commentary (Matthew), Pilgrim Aflame* (a historical novel, now in film, "The Radicals," *Soli Deo Gloria: A Daily Devotional through Romans,* and *The Christ-Shaped Conscience.*

Introduction

SPIRITUAL LIFE IS DEPENDENT UPON the function of the Holy Spirit *upon, within,* and *through* the life of the believer. Many persons who profess the Christian faith are unacquainted with the Spirit and His redemptive work. For this reason, the church in general is falling far short of the perfection of Christ. Only a proper relationship to the Holy Spirit can correct our problems of carnality, selfishness, and worldliness. The church must actually become a "dwelling place of God in the Spirit."

The chapters of this book are not deep theological treatises, but are rather practical biblical discussions concerning sins against the Holy Spirit. It is my prayer that the Holy Spirit will use these chapters to promote a revival of personal commitment to the lordship of Christ and of His gracious Spirit. As you read the book, may you avoid a mere evaluation of the theories regarding the Spirit's work, and open yourself for a new infilling of the Holy Spirit. If you will make your approach a devotional one, God will do a gracious work of spiritual renewal within your soul.

Seven definite terms are used in the New Testament to designate various types of sins against the Holy Spirit. The following chapters are discussions of these seven sins against the Spirit. To them I have added two opening chapters and two concluding chapters. Several of these chapters deal with difficult passages in the Bible concerning which there is difference of opinion, influenced by varied theological systems. I have attempted to be objective and true to the context in treating these passages.

In fairness to the reader, I believe in the security of the believer conditionally, not unconditionally. There is security in Christ, but not in sin. As we abide in Him, so He abides in us to seal and safeguard our spiritual relationship through the presence of His Spirit. As the warnings against disbelief are addressed to Christians in the Epistle to the Hebrews, so a discussion on "Sins Against the Spirit" must take into account the danger this sin brings to the Christian experience. Sins against the Spirit violate the conditions of this abiding fellowship. Our security is one of relationship with Christ as Lord.

In studying the person and work of the Spirit, it must be remembered that He came to glorify Christ. The Spirit-filled life is one in which Christ is preeminent. A balanced Christian faith will seek to share in the threefold emphasis of Paul in Ephesians: the fullness of God, the fullness of Christ, and the fullness of the Spirit. I commend to you a life that is "complete in him" as you meditate on these chapters.

Acknowledgment should here be given to those unnamed sources on which I have drawn from memory. A word of thanks is also due Elizabeth and Janet Kreider for their efficient work as typists and their editorial suggestions. A further acknowledgement of thanks is here expressed to J. C. Wenger, of Goshen Biblical Seminary, Elkhart Seminary, Elkhart, Indiana, for reading the manuscript.

Myron S. Augsburger

CHAPTER 1

The Transforming Spirit

Paul ... came to Ephesus. There he found some disciples.
And he said to them, "Did you receive the Holy Spirit when
you believed?" And they said, "No, we have never even
heard that there is a Holy Spirit."
Acts 19:1-2

A PASTOR INVITED A YOUNG MAN to become a Christian and
received the reply, "Religion for my grandfather was an experience,
for my father it was a tradition, and for me it is a nuisance." Too
often we have left out the experiential aspect of walking with
Christ. Many professing Christians are ignorant of the Holy Spirit
and His work. We live in a Pentecost age, but many have a pre-
Pentecost experience. Every believer should know the full joy of
abiding in Christ and of His indwelling presence.

The church is to be a "dwelling place of God in the Spirit" (Eph. 2:22). One of the serious failures of the church is that of
ignorance of the person, presence, and work of the Holy Spirit. A
prominent theologian, Newbigin of South India, has said that the
church of the twentieth century needs to rediscover the meaning of
separation from the world and the meaning of Pentecost! The
church tends to become institutionalized, formalized, and secular-
ized. For many people, joining church is on the same level as joining a club, and may be done for business and social advantages ra-

ther than as a spiritual experience and expression.

The church, as it involves individual believers and the corporate body, must know His dynamic presence. No group can ever become a spiritually disciplined church without honoring the Holy Spirit. He is God's means of manifesting the lordship of Christ over contemporary believers. Spiritual authority resides in the mind of Christ, and we come to understand the mind of Christ through the Word and the Holy Spirit.

We need to discover how to say, "It seemed good to the Holy Spirit and to us" (Acts 15:28). Instead of this New Testament pattern we have the order reversed. We plan our program and then ask divine blessing upon our plans. As one person put it, "We know where we are going in the next five years and we hope it pleases the Holy Spirit to go along."

The Holy Spirit is God's executive in the world and God's agent in redemption. He has been active in creating and sustaining the universe. He is active in convicting and converting men to God, in correcting and in sanctifying the lives of believers, and in anointing and empowering those in God's service. The unique aspect of the Spirit's work in the New Testament, in contrast to the Old, is witnessing to the finished work of the Lord Jesus Christ. The provision of the gospel, in forgiveness of sin and a new life in Christ, is confirmed by His indwelling presence. This is the satisfaction of which Jesus said, "If any one thirst, let him come to me and drink.... 'Out of his heart shall flow rivers of living [satisfying] water'" (John 7:37-38).

In the account of Acts 19 we find Paul asking some disciples at Ephesus the personal question, "Did you receive the Holy Spirit?" The question here is not a question of time, but a question of reality. Apparently he asked this question because it appeared that their experience was inadequate. It soon became apparent that their knowledge of the Holy Spirit was also inadequate. They must have known about the work of the Holy Spirit in the Old Testament setting, having an intellectual belief in the Messiah through John the Baptist.

However, up to this point they did not know that the Holy Spirit was being received by individual believers. They did not know that their Messiah had died, risen from the dead, ascended to heaven as Lord and Christ, and as His first regal act had given the gift of the Holy Spirit to His own. When Paul asked them concerning this experiential aspect of their faith in Christ as Lord, he found their experience inadequate.

Today also persons must not only have an intellectual understanding of Jesus as Messiah, but need to make an individual commitment to Christ as Lord. When Christ is acknowledged as Lord of our life, He has moral freedom to send the Holy Spirit to reside and rule in the life of His own. One cause for spiritual anemia in the lives of many believers is ignorance about the Spirit and His purpose.

Numerous scriptural terms designate great spiritual experiences which Christians are privileged to enjoy. Christianity needs to be understood to be more fully experienced. Experience with Christ goes far beyond intellectual considerations, but it does not happen apart from the conscious insight of the mind. Let's consider several basic biblical terms which lie at the heart of the gospel. In understanding and experiencing their meaning there is real joy and victory.

The Regeneration of the Holy Spirit

In Jesus' interview with Nicodemus He startled the religious world forever by saying, "Unless one is born of water and the Spirit, he cannot enter the kingdom of God" (John 3:8). When Jesus said, "You must be born anew" (John 3:7), He was speaking of a spiritual birth. Man was created as a spiritual being, but having revolted against God he is described by the Bible as spiritually dead. Persons without Christ have an "amputated ... personality with the top plane missing."[1]

In his revolt against God, man's spirit broke from the rule of God's Spirit. Instead of man being governed by spiritual fellowship with God, man is controlled by the soul or self-conscious aspect of his being. Man's basic sin is egoism, a life under the control of self. A little atheism in the heart of every man tends to replace God with self at the center of one's life.

Understood in this light, self-effort in religion is sinful at its source because it is man erecting his own pattern in opposition to God's provision. Man's religious practices can never bring him into a saving relationship with God, because they are aspects of his own self-will. Jesus was speaking to a religious man, orthodox and conservative in his theology, exacting and obedient to his ideals, and yet Jesus said, "You must be born anew."

Being born anew, as expressed in the New Testament, is passive grammatically, meaning that we do not accomplish this ourselves. We do not give birth to ourselves, but rather we receive new life as a gift. Man is free to make his own decisions, but he comes into God's grace only as the Spirit draws him. Responding to God's invitation by faith, man experiences a new birth. In this experience man's dead spirit is made alive by the Holy Spirit, and operates under the control of God's Spirit thus making him a new person in Christ Jesus. Just as there is a definite time when one is born physically, so the new birth means that there is a definite moment when one begins a spiritual life.

The Spirit witnesses to the full salvation within the heart (Rom. 8:16). It is the believer's privilege to rest in the assurance that he is a born-again child of God. We do not have a hope-so salvation, but a salvation which gives hope. There is no uncertainty in the heart of one who is saved regarding his relationship with Christ. Of this definiteness Bryan Green has said, "You know whether your face or your back is toward God."[2] The Scripture says, "He who has the Son has life; he who has not the Son of God has not life" (1 John 5:12).

The Baptism with the Holy Spirit

The New Testament refers to the Holy Spirit working upon, within, and through the life of the believer. Just as conviction and regeneration were aspects of the Spirit's operation upon man's heart, now the baptism with the Holy Spirit is that initial aspect of the Spirit's dwelling within man's heart. Regeneration is the occasion when the Holy Spirit makes man's dead spirit alive, while the baptism with the Holy Spirit is a divine presence which energizes man's new relation with His Lord. The baptism with the Holy Spirit is that occasion when Jesus gives the Holy Spirit to those who accept Him as Lord.

It is significant to note that the preposition used in the Bible concerning this experience is not "of" but "with." There are those who speak of a baptism "of" the Spirit as though this is something the Holy Spirit gives to one in special energizing for witness. There

5

is an anointing of the Spirit for power and witness which will be discussed later. Let us not confuse these terms and thereby under-emphasize the meaning of being baptized "with" the Holy Spirit.

The One doing the baptizing is the Lord Himself, and the baptism is with the Holy Spirit. The Holy Spirit Himself is the baptism in this experience! The new birth makes one spiritually alive, while this baptism with the Holy Spirit is the presence of the Spirit uniting this new life with Christ. This is a unique aspect of the conversion experience and to be honored on its own merit. John the Baptist said, "I baptize you with water for repentance, but he who is coming after me is mightier than I, whose sandals I am not worthy to carry; he will baptize you with the Holy Spirit and with fire" (Matt. 3:11). Jesus reemphasized this promise, stating, "For John baptized with water, but before many days you shall be baptized with the Holy Spirit.... But you shall receive power when the Holy Spirit has come upon you: and you shall be my witnesses in Jerusalem and in all Judea and Samaria and to the end of the earth" (Acts 1:5, 8).

As John closes his Gospel, it is not without mention of the promised gift of the Holy Spirit. Throughout the Gospel of John there are many references to the work of the Holy Spirit who would be given when Jesus was glorified. Now in John 20:22, as Jesus was preparing to go to the Father and share His glory, He said to the disciples, "Receive the Holy Spirit." In the Greek language this is in the imperative, which means, "You must receive the Holy Ghost." Jesus was pointing to Pentecost and preparing the disciples for that great spiritual experience.

Each of us must ask if the reality and meaning of this experience is present in his life. Might it be that we have only a head knowledge about Christ as God's Son, our Savior? Have we missed out on the personal experience with Him as Savior and Lord? Much of popular Christianity seems to be an "insurance policy" to guarantee missing hell and gaining heaven, but is not interested in living a life of quality under the lordship of Christ here and now.

Paul stated the condition for salvation: "That if thou shalt confess Jesus as Lord, and believe in thine heart that he is a living Lord that you are going to serve, you shall be saved."[3] Thus Paul emphasized that Jesus becomes Savior by being our Lord. Those persons who would like a Savior but who do not want a Lord are missing out on the meaning of Christ's redemptive work. When one commits his life to Christ as Lord, Jesus is given the right to exercise His lordship through the Holy Spirit.[4]

We have observed that the objective side of the baptism with the Holy Spirit is the occasion when Jesus gives the Holy Spirit to the believer confessing Christ as Lord. Let us now look at the subjective side, or the meaning of this baptism in the life of the believer.

The term "baptism" means to be brought under control of a superior power or influence. It is so used with respect to various types of baptism in the New Testament. Being baptized with fire means to be brought under the control or influence of a judging, cleansing process. Being baptized with suffering means to be brought under the control or influence of a suffering experience. Being baptized into the church, or into the body of Christ, means to be brought under the control and influence of the body of the church. And being baptized with the Holy Spirit means to be brought under the control of His superior power and influence.

The baptism with the Spirit is thus a crisis experience when the believing heart commits the believer to Christ as Lord and comes under the control of His Spirit. Christ is justly given the privilege of controlling that life, since it is committed to Him. The baptism with the Spirit is not simply a historical event, nor is it something that only rests upon the church as a corporate body, but is rather the individual believer's experience of receiving the Holy Spirit to control his life and guide it in the way of holiness.

One shares in the church through being in Christ, rather than the opposite view which is held by some churches. It is through this experience that one is identified with Christ in a manner which accomplishes the crucifixion of the old life. Many persons fail to enjoy the fullness of this privilege. Because they do not understand this great truth, they are not able to claim its benefits by faith. Others fail to enter into the full meaning of this new life because they draw back from the "death route," the experience of dying to self in being crucified with Christ.

The Sealing with the Spirit

The Bible says, "The Lord knows those who are his" (2 Tim. 2:19). One who is regenerated and baptized with the Spirit is spoken of as "sealed with the promised Holy Spirit" (Eph. 1:13). Again Paul says, "But it is God who establishes us with you in Christ, and has commissioned us; he has put his seal upon us ... (2 Cor. 1:21-22). This term "seal" refers to ownership. An illustration is found in the seal of a country, such as the United States seal, which places the object under all the rights and protection of that country. It is significant to note that Paul says it is God who seals the believer. Again, we are sealed, not by the Spirit, but "with the Spirit." The presence of the Spirit in the believer's life is the guarantee that he belongs to God. Paul says, "It is the Spirit himself bearing witness with our spirit, that we are children of God" (Rom. 8:16).

Further, the evidence of the Spirit within our lives, as seen in the fruit of the Spirit, is the guarantee to those about us that we are of God. However, the greater meaning of this seal relates to our security in Christ. In being sealed through the Spirit's presence we are kept from the power of Satan. John speaks of our victory over evil spirits, saying, "Little children, you are of God and have overcome them; for he who is in you is greater than he who is in the world" (1 John 4:4). As to our responsibility of yielding to the Spirit to make this security effective, John adds, "We know that any one born of God does not sin, but He who was born of God keeps him, and the evil one does not touch him" (1 John 5:18).

The security of the believer is one of the rich teachings of the New Testament. This is a security in Christ, not in sin. This security is not a mechanical relationship with Christ which cannot be revoked or undone. It is a security of quality. The quality of the relationship in Christ is infinitely superior to the former life in sin. One in Christ has found the ultimate satisfaction for which his heart longs. This security is spoken of in John, 10:27-30, when Jesus said, "My sheep hear my voice, and I know them, and they follow me; and I give them eternal life, and they shall never perish, and no one shall snatch them out of my hand. My Father, who has given them to me, is greater than all, and no one is able to snatch them out of the Father's hand."

The condition of this security is stated in verse 27, "My sheep hear my voice, and I know them, and they follow me." The person who is following Christ has a right to claim this seal of the Spirit. The presence of the Spirit is the seal that one belongs to God. Only the person who is following Christ, or as Paul expresses it, walking in the Spirit, has a valid seal upon his life.

One who abides in Christ has no question about his relationship with Christ today nor his eternal destiny. The Christian has the confidence that he will live with God as long as God lives! This security is ours because of the promise of God and the witness of His Spirit. As one walks in the Spirit and has respect for His will, this seal remains unbroken.

The idea of conditional security need not cause one to fear. A good illustration is in the conditional security of marriage. Just because of the possibility that a marriage may break up, the couple need not live in fear that it will happen. Rather, they practice those attitudes of love which enrich the relationship.[5]

All spiritual blessings which come into the life of the believer or the church come by way of the Spirit. Jesus introduced Him as a person and as a member of the Godhead. In this divine Trinity there is identity, distinction, and equality. The Holy Spirit is the expression of God in this age, confirming the plan of the Father and the provision of Christ. He has come to glorify Christ, and accomplishes His work in the believer and through him.

As a person, the Spirit can be acknowledged and accepted or spurned and rejected. G. Campbell Morgan emphasizes the characteristics of personality. "Four things are contained within the realm of personality—Will, Intelligence, Power, and Capacity for Love. A person is a being who can be approached, trusted or doubted, loved or hated, adored or insulted. These essential parts of personality are limited in human beings: the will has its limitations."[6]

God calls, but does not coerce. The Spirit does not force Himself into a person's life but awaits recognition and response. Confronted with the work of the Spirit, one can either accept or reject, honor or disregard Him. The church needs to open its heart to this supernatural, dynamic power that will energize its ministry and mission. Only in knowing His presence do we have the dynamic power that creates the true church. The church exists where the living Christ is present in the person of the Holy Spirit witnessing to believing hearts.

The effect of the Spirit's work is to create a community of believers. The individual shares in the church by virtue of being "in Christ," and in turn is enabled to better perceive Christ in the context of the church. Although faith is the experience of the individual, it cannot be fully enjoyed as an individual. Man is never his best when he stands alone, and so the believer is never fully aware of the grandeur of Christ without the church. One who comes to God "in Christ" comes to appreciate his brother "in Christ." Any sin against the unity of the brotherhood is a sin against the Spirit creating this unity.

CHAPTER 2

The Sanctifying Spirit

Do you not know that your body is a temple of the Holy Spirit within you, which you have from God? You are not your own; you were bought with a price. So glorify God in your body.

1 Corinthians 6:19-20

GOD HAS A REDEMPTIVE CLAIM upon the believer's life. One who understands the meaning of Calvary becomes aware that he is purchased at a great price, and in response to Christ becomes the property of Another. God is not primarily interested in one's religion, praise, or service, but in the individual. God does not want your religion; He wants you! The Spirit of God within the life of the believer is there to validate and venerate the divine claim upon the personality of man. Ours is not a God far removed, but one who has moved into the heart of our experience.

The sanctifying work of the Spirit is the conscious outworking of this divine possession. God has said, "You shall be holy; for I am holy" (1 Pet. 1:16). The basis of holiness is the sovereignty of God as Lord of the world. God asks the believer to yield his life to the Spirit who will conform his basic motivations to the will of Christ. This begins with the awareness that one is "chosen in Christ" to be God's possession. Brunner says "a thing is holy because, and in so far as, it is His property and is recognized as such. The holiness of

13

man consists in knowing that he belongs to God."[1]

We need always to be honest about our sinfulness as we share in His holiness. God accepts sinners on the basis of His own grace. The call of grace asks us to be repentant in mind and responsive in heart. The story is told of a widow who raised one son, sent him through Cambridge, and later saw him off to the service of her country. His death in active service was a crushing blow. One night she dreamed that an angel came and offered her the privilege of having her son back for five minutes at any stage of his life. She decided not to ask for him as a college graduate, or as a man among men, but instead as the disobedient boy who ran out into the garden angry, only to return and throw himself sobbing into her arms in repentance. This is the way God wants us, and it is the only way we can come from our way of sin to share in His holiness.

Holiness is the absence of sin, and thus we share in His holiness as we share in the cleansing power of the blood of Christ. As long as we operate in the human sphere we share in the limitations of human nature. Therefore, our experience of holiness is (1) imputed in the forgiveness of His grace; (2) it is implanted in the sense of the presence of the divine Spirit indwelling the believer; and (3) it is imparted depending on the degree to which the ethic of Christ's love directs the believer's life. Being partakers of His holiness is a matter of enjoying the benefits of His presence, and the guidance of His voice.

The sanctifying work of the Spirit deals with the very core of life. It is not some code of behavior which one adopts and then claims a status above his fellows in grace. Holiness means that one has become God's possession at the very heart of his existence, that "inner man" which calls the signals of life. The work of the Spirit within one leads first to the basic commitment of death to the "old man," a definite cessation of the old pattern of life. Secondly it leads to the creating and preserving of the "new man," meaning the Spirit's control of the new life. This experience of the divine presence brings the "I" - "Thou" relation into the heart of individual response.

In addition to the several terms discussed in the preceding chapter, which are the basis for the transforming experience of sanctification, we will discuss four terms in this chapter which are the cause for the transformed expression of sanctification. These are (1) the experience of divine presence, or "the guarantee of the Spirit"; (2) the experience of divine power, or the anointing of the Spirit; (3) the experience of divine possession, or the filling of the Spirit; and (4) the experience of the divine purpose, or the communion of the Spirit. The wonder of His grace is not only seen in the justification of the sinner, but in the crucifixion of the old life and the creation of the new man.

The Guarantee of the Spirit

The Christian life is a qualify of life infinitely superior to the life in sin. The new life in Christ is to be nonconformed to the former life in sin. As believers we become members of the heavenly kingdom and have been translated from the kingdom of darkness into the kingdom of His dear Son. We live as strangers and pilgrims here and are, in fact, citizens of heaven even while we live in this world. The Bible says, "As he is so are we in this world" (1 John 4:17). While living here, we are in truth walking with God. This is God the Holy Spirit dwelling within, permeating, sanctifying, transforming the life of the believer. In fellowship with Christ we are already enjoying a foretaste of the glories which shall be hereafter.

In 1 Corinthians 1:9-10, Paul states that "no eye has seen, nor ear heard, nor the heart of man conceived, what God has prepared for those who love him." Yet he adds, "God has revealed [these] to us through the Spirit." Through the presence of the Spirit of God at work we have a foretaste of glory.

Of this foretaste of glory Paul states that not only are we sealed with the Spirit, but He has "given us his Spirit in our hearts as a guarantee" (2 Cor. 2:23). In conversion we have made a covenant commitment with Christ, and as a guarantee of the full glory we shall someday share in His presence. He has already given us the Holy Spirit. Paul, speaking of our present pilgrimage and our anxiety about life after death, speaks of God as having "given to us the Spirit as a guarantee" (2 Cor. 5:5). In the Ephesian letter he is more explicit, adding that the Holy Spirit is the guarantee of our inheritance until we acquire possession of it, "to the praise of his glory" (Eph. 1:14).

The presence of the Spirit in our lives is the foretaste of the heavenly glory of being with God, for He is God with us now. In the Old Testament the Shekinah glory of God's presence lighted the tabernacle, but now He counts each believer as a temple of the Holy Spirit. At Pentecost the Shekinah glory-cloud filled the room, then broke into little tongues of flame which came to rest on each head. The Spirit is the present experience of divine glory and presence, to be fully shared in the final consummation of eternal glory.

The Anointing of the Spirit

Another term used in the New Testament to describe an aspect of the Spirit's work is anointing. This manifestation of the Spirit is often discussed as a "baptism of the Spirit" to the exclusion of His other work in a believer's life. In looking at terms we are not primarily concerned about any stipulated order. In fact, to speak about the order of the Spirit's working within a person's life is not fair to the interrelation between the human personality and the divine personality.

In God's grace, He always meets a man where he is. One dare not make his ow experience the yardstick by which he measures the experience of other people, It makes almost as much sense to debate which spoke moves first when a wheel begins to turn, as to argue about the order in which God's Spirit will work in the believer's life. Many aspects of the Spirit's work may be simultaneous and overlap. The designations used here are simply an attempt to point up that these are not synonymous, and that each term carries a meaning of its own.

The term "anointing" is used throughout the Bible to designate God's selection, equipping, and empowering of a man for particular service. With respect to the anointing of the Spirit upon Christ, Chester K. Lehman states, "God's anointing Jesus with the Spirit brought upon Jesus the fullness of divine power. Throughout His earthly life the Spirit was the Energizer. It was the anointing of the Spirit that made Jesus the Anointed One, the Messiah. This anointing energized Christ for his threefold mission: (1) Jesus was the Anointed Prophet who proclaimed the 'good tidings'; (2) He was the Anointed High Priest who 'made purification for sins'; (3) He was the Anointed King who '[reigns] in righteousness.' He who heightened Jesus' powers in this three-fold ministry was the Holy Spirit."[2]

At Jesus' baptism the Spirit of God came upon Him. Immediately following His baptism, the Holy Spirit led Jesus into the wilderness, to clarify His role as Messiah-Redeemer in the program of

God's redeeming grace. During this time Jesus was confronted by Satan in temptation of the most severe nature. Under the anointing of the Holy Spirit, He had power both to discern and to defeat these attacks. Returning to His home village at Nazareth, He was asked to read the Scripture in the synagogue. In Luke 4, Jesus read His testimony from Isaiah 61:1, saying, "The Spirit of the Lord is upon me, because he has anointed me to preach good news to the poor." Clearly, "anointing" is a word symbolizing divine commission, authority, and power. Peter emphasized in Acts 10:36 "how God anointed Jesus of Nazareth with the Holy Spirit and with power; how he went about doing good and healing all that were oppressed by the devil, for God was with him."

The anointing is thus a symbol of God's empowering and commissioning one as a witness. Paul applies this to us in the words, "But it is God who establishes us with you in Christ, and has commissioned [anointed] us" (2 Cor. 1:21). Throughout the ministry of Christ, His preaching was accompanied with spiritual works as a direct result of the anointing with the Spirit. The Bible says the Spirit was given without measure to Him. This same anointing is to be experienced by the believer through the provision of Christ.

This practical application or the privilege resulting from this anointing is spiritual insight. Jesus said, "He will guide you into ell the truth'" (John 16:13). John writes, "But you have been anointed by the Holy One, and you all know [spiritual] things" (John 2:20). Under the Spirit's anointing each believer has the perception to discern spiritual things. To make this clearer, he adds in his discussion of how believers discern false teachers. "But the anointing which you received from him abides in you and you have no need that any one should teach you; as his anointing teaches you about everything and is no lie, and just as it has taught you, abide in him" (1 John

2:27). Hence the believer who is sensitive to the voice of the Spirit can discern whether a thing is consistent with the nature of Christ or not.

This anointing of the Spirit is greatly needed today. The gifts of the Spirit referred to in 1 Corinthians 12 and 14 include a gift of discernment. There is great need in these days of apostasy for spiritual discernment. We need to discern how the Spirit of God is leading. In these times we must have a "word from the Lord," a prophetic voice, forthtelling, making the gospel relevant in today's situation. It is this anointing of the Spirit which enables a man of Cod to present the Word with power to change lives.

The Filling of the Spirit

God's work of redemption is that of making saints out of sinners. Once life was self-oriented; now it is Christ-oriented. Where once life was filled with selfish ambitions, now it is filled with spiritual aspirations. Where once life was warped by the pursuits of the sensual, now it is warmed by the presence of the Spirit. Where once life was possessed by the vainglories of the human ego, now in Christ it is possessed by the person of the Holy Spirit. Paul describes the believer's position by the phrase "in Christ," the relationship through which we enjoy all the benefits of Spirit-possession.

This word is one which describes experience. We are commanded by Paul in Ephesians 5:18 to "be filled with the Spirit." In Acts 2 we find the disciples filled with the Spirit in the same experience as their reception of the Spirit. It must also be noted that in Acts 4 these same disciples who had been filled were filled anew. It is also significant that reference is made to men, such as Stephen,

Philip, and Peter, "being full of the Holy Spirit." The term appears to describe the experiential relation between the yielded heart and the Holy Spirit. That a person has received the Holy Spirit is no guarantee that he is at a given time filled with the Spirit. The baptism with the Spirit is the crisis experience when He is given to the believer, while the filling of the Spirit is the continual experience of His possessing the believer. There is one baptism of the Spirit, but many fillings.

The term "filled" could be translated "possessed." The Spirit-filled life, or Spirit-possessed life, is not one in which we have a certain amount of the Spirit, but rather one in which He possesses all of us. The Spirit-filled life is one in which the Spirit expresses Himself within an individual as a controlling and overflowing force. The condition is one of yieldedness on our part. We are as filled with the Spirit as we are emptied of self. Since yieldedness is a voluntary attitude, it follows that we are just as filled with the Spirit as we want to be.

The meaning of a Spirit-filled life, or a Spirit-possessed life is illustrated in an incident concerning D. L. Moody. He was invited to conduct a city-wide evangelistic crusade and the local ministry had met in planning. One of the ministers who didn't believe strongly in this type of evangelistic mission asked, "Why must we get D. L. Moody to come here? Does he have a monopoly on the Holy Spirit?" Another minister aptly replied, "No, D. L. Moody doesn't have a monopoly on the Holy Spirit, but the Holy Spirit has a monopoly on D. L. Moody." The Spirit-possessed life is one of deliberate abandonment of one's self to the Holy Spirit.

The fullness of the Spirit is in proportion to our conscious yieldedness to His will. This is the believer's responsibility. In grace, there are some aspects where the believer is passive. We are to "be" born again, we are to "be" filled with the Spirit, we are to "be" sanctified. These are spiritual realities which God implements. On the other hand, there are aspects of grace where we are active, thereby making it possible for God to implement the former. We are to repent, we are to believe, we are to yield, we are to consecrate, and we are to obey! The Spirit-filled life is contingent upon our active response to His will.

The Communion of the Holy Spirit

This term, coming from Paul's benediction in 2 Corinthians 13:14 (KJV), expresses both the idea of the Comforter or Counselor as spoken of by Christ (John 14:26; 16:7-14), and of the leading of the Spirit as found in Romans 8. The communion of the Spirit is that privilege of spiritual exchange in meditation by which the mind of Christ is discerned. As a Comforter, Jesus meant one who stands alongside in full understanding and concern, the Paraclete. Paul adds that understanding the spiritual warfare in which the believer is engaged, the Spirit prays for us, or engages in the spiritual exchange with heaven, which brings God's power to bear against the opposing forces of evil, and quickens our limited strength.

It also follows that in communion with the Spirit, we are led of the Spirit. Paul says, "For all who are led by the Spirit of God are sons of God" (Rom. 8:14). Such people live in communion with the Spirit. A believer has the privilege of divine leading if he will quiet his heart in deference to the voice of the Spirit. A challenging illustration is in the case of Philip, in Acts 8, who was led by the Spirit to meet and witness to the Ethiopian eunuch. So we ought to be sensitive to the prompting of the Spirit, to respond to His direction as He promotes kingdom interests in the world.

One of the great blessings of the communion of the Spirit is that of finding in this relationship the position and the power for victory. In Galatians 5 we discover that as we live in the Spirit and walk in the Spirit, He is able to produce in and through us the fruit of the Spirit. Our responsibility is outlined in these words, "But I say, walk by the Spirit, and do not gratify the desires of the flesh. For the desires of the flesh are against the Spirit, and the desires of the Spirit are against the flesh; for these are opposed to each other, to prevent you from doing what you would" (Gal. 5:16-17). The verbs in these two verses are in the present tense in the Greek, which means that this is a process of relationship. The Word "flesh" could here be translated "self." The self continually desires to go its way and the Spirit continually desires to go His way, and these two are continually contrary the one to the other. However, the great conclusion is found in the statement that the Spirit is always there "to prevent you from doing what you would"!

The Holy Spirit's presence keeps one from following the desire of the self. Pick up a book. Hold it out from your body and notice the pull of gravity which draws it down. Yet it cannot fall because you overcome the pull of gravity and support it. Since you are many times stronger than the pull of gratify in the book, it cannot fall because you lift it. In like manner, within the life of the believer it is possible for the self-life to go against God. But because of the sanctifying, indwelling presence of the Holy Spirit, He is there counteracting the tendency to go against God. This means that by His presence one is prevented from doing the thing that he would have done had the Spirit of God not been present. Thus by the continuous presence of the Holy Spirit, there is both provision and power for victory.

For many persons the Spirit is merely an impersonal force operating in the world. For others the Spirit of Christ means merely the nature or attitudes of Christ as they are imitated in the professing Christian church. For others the Spirit is the presence of God in the corporate body of the church without any personal indwelling. The latter are those who teach that we only share in the Spirit as we share in the corporate group and thus partake of His influence. Few are those believers who have a dynamic faith in the personal indwelling of the Holy Spirit within the individual life. Such lack of insight into His work means that many Christians sin against the Spirit by simply being ignorant of His person and purpose.

Many have only a religion of confessing sins and claiming Christ as Savior from their burden of guilt, but they have missed the positive, creating, energizing power of the presence of the Spirit. Others have a well-outlined philosophy of Christian religion, including forgiveness of sins, reconciliation to God, and an imitation of Christ, but they have no power to live for Christ. Such persons know nothing of regeneration, of identification with Christ, and of participation in His holiness, all through the presence and power of the Holy Spirit.

It is not enough merely to know intellectually who the Holy Spirit is as a person. It is not sufficient to understand intellectually those doctrinal aspects of His work. The work of the Holy Spirit is to be personal and dynamic, experiential and transforming. Each believer must claim by faith the subjective aspects of these great truths. Until the Spirit of God is known as a person who dwells within one's life, creating, transforming, and energizing, one has missed the fullness of God's grace. If one would know the fullness of His transforming presence, he must meet the conditions outlined in Acts 5:32 in the words of Peter: "the Holy Spirit whom God has given to those who obey him."

CHAPTER 3

Resisting the Spirit

"You stiff-necked people, uncircumcised in heart and ears,
you always resist the Holy Spirit."
Acts 7:51

ONE OF MAN'S CHIEF SINS is to resist God. The Holy Spirit is the executive of the Godhead at work in the world. Through Him a sovereign God moves upon the hearts of men, that He might bring faith to birth. Resisting the Spirit is to oppose the eternal work of God as it bears upon one's own soul. This attitude is a continuation of man's revolt against God, separating man from God in a state of spiritual death. It is in this sense that man's greatest potential, the freedom to make moral decisions, becomes his greatest downfall. God has given man the power to talk back to Him, and man's sin is that he has "sassed God off."

One of the most pointed sermons in the Bible is Acts 7, where Stephen addresses the religious men his day and exposes their sin of resisting the Holy Spirit. These men were really not in search of truth, they had a doctrine of a sovereign God, but they would not let Him be sovereign. They had sacrificed the person of God for mere precepts about God. Their search for truth failed because they had forgotten the transcendent goal. They made the mistake of looking at some immediate selfish goal rather than at the eternal spiritual goal.

Their preoccupation with a minor goal reminds one of the young boy scout who met with his group. When the scoutmaster asked if all had done their good deed for the day, everyone raised his hand except one little lad. He was asked, according to their rules, to leave until the good deed was accomplished. About twenty minutes later he was back with a big smile, but his hair was tousled and his clothes torn. He told the scoutmaster that he had tried to help an old lady across the street, but she didn't want to go!

The real goal is not religious practice but the reality of His presence. Man must always remember that God is larger than any system of thought or doctrine. Man's mind is closed to truth as it was revealed in Christ because the sinfulness of man's heart reacts to the person of His holiness. The man who hates divine truth does so because of the evil in his own life. Wrapped up in our religious program, we do not realize that what is really important is what happens inside us, not outside us. Stephen summed up his message to the resisting Pharisees, "You always resist the Holy Spirit." They had closed their minds to God's unfolding revelation.

Resisting the Spirit is a common sin in the experience of mankind, among both the irreligious and the religious. To resist means to oppose, to stand against, or to withstand. It is man's opposition to God's redemptive measures on his behalf. It is man's refusal to share in full reconciliation to God. It is man's choice to retain sin even at the cost of losing fellowship with God. Resisting the Spirit is to stand in opposition to God's program of making saints out of sinners.

Rejecting the Spirit's Convicting Call

God's evangelist in the world is the Holy Spirit. He is using many believers as channels through whom He works. Believers testify to the reality of grace, but it is the Spirit who transforms one through divine grace. Man may convince the mind through building a case for Christian faith, but it is only the Spirit who convicts the man. Men may confront others with the gospel, but only the Holy. Spirit can convert them to the gospel.

Whenever the church magnifies its program above the person of Christ and its platform above the power of the Spirit, it has sinned against the work of Christ. The Spirit is God's evangelist in the world, using men as tools to lift up Christ. Whenever a program or tradition displaces Christ, the Spirit is hindered in His work. For this reason, God writes "Ichabod" over many doors, for the glory of the Lord has departed. We cannot expect to win souls to Christ when the church has become merely a social association with religious bylaws. The church must be a body of redeemed sinners through whom the Spirit witnesses of Christ.

One of the greatest favors God does any man is to call him by the Holy Spirit. Jesus said, "No one can come to me unless the Father who sent me draws him" (John 6:44). The Spirit of God is at work calling men to faith in Christ. Of this call Jesus said that many are called but few are chosen (Matt. 20:16 KJV). Our being chosen in him is contingent upon our response to the Spirit's call. It is when man, by voluntary choice, responds to the call of the Spirit that he is brought into a living fellowship with Christ. God, through His foreknowledge, thus speaks of us as having been chosen "in him before the foundation of the world, that we should be holy and blameless before him" (Ephesians 1:4). Man resists the Spirit when he rejects this call, and thus brings upon himself the responsibility for his lost condition outside of Christ.

The call of the Spirit is a gracious invitation for the sinner to renounce the way of self and turn to Christ. The conscience, by its very nature of passing judgment on one's behavior on the basis of acquired knowledge, is primarily a negative voice. The call of the Spirit is primarily a positive voice. One may, as did Paul, live in harmony with his conscience in not violating his religious precepts, and yet not come to God. It is the positive call of the Spirit that leads one not only to renounce sin, but to turn to Christ.

One may have a deep feeling of conviction for his violations of conscience, and be emotionally broken up over his sin, yet not come to peace in Christ. It is only as one answers the Spirit's positive call of commitment to Christ that he has peace with God. It not enough to confess sin; one must confess Christ, as Savior and Lord. One may confess sin without confessing Christ, but one cannot truly confess Christ as Lord without also confessing sin.

The conscience is the God-given channel by which the Spirit convicts man. Convictions vary in individuals because of the many differences in their traditions and training, culture and comprehension. The conscience, however, speaks consistently to all men of every culture at one point. Regardless of the validity of their claim to know right from wrong, the conscience witnesses by its vote on the side of what they think is right, that there is something within calling them to the best. Thinking man, created in the image of God, is thereby challenged to pursue the search for truth.

The conscience is not the standard; it is to be standardized by God's Word. Conscience is really a God-given servant, not a grueling master. As Christians we dare not ignore the voice nor violate the will of conscience, but we can change the conscience by educating it in divine truth! The Holy Spirit stands ready to guide the believer in this inner renewal of the mind. Paul speaks of this in Romans 12:2: "Do not be not conformed to this world but be transformed by the renewal of your mind, that you may prove what is the will of God, what is good and acceptable and perfect."

Many times a person under the conviction of the Holy Spirit is greatly troubled; but the troubled heart is due to our lack of yield-edness rather than to the nature of the Spirit's call. The Spirit is not primarily interested in making a person miserable; yet when the Spirit calls and man resists, there is the misery of a "civil war" within. The gracious call of the Holy Spirit is an invitation to the abundant life in Christ, with all its joy, peace, and spiritual pleas-ure. The misery in the convicted soul is due to man's resisting the Spirit and continuing his revolt against God. Peace of heart comes when man, through the Spirit, is brought into a spiritual relation with the Lord, described in Romans 6 as yieldedness.

Rejecting the Spirit's Revelation of Truth

In John 14 and 16 Jesus refers to the Holy Spirit as the "Spirit of truth." He declares that the Spirit will "guide you into all the truth." Paul states in 1 Corinthians 2:10, that what the natural man cannot perceive the believer understands because "God has re-vealed [it] to us through the Spirit." John makes clear in his First Epistle that it is by the anointing of the Holy Spirit that "we all un-derstand spiritual things" (1 John 2:20, literal translation). Hence, we conclude that only by the Spirit's inspiration can the mind of man comprehend spiritual things. The written Word becomes "spirit and life" (John 6:63) as this Spirit makes it a living, pulsing, creating power within the soul.

One resists the Spirit when he refuses to exchange human opin-ions for heaven-sent convictions. Opinion is what a man thinks on an issue, while conviction is man's belief of truth. There is no valid conviction but that which is based on divine revelation. One who is open to the Spirit is ready to add hew convictions to his life as he understands the Bible. Such a person is willing to accept new truths, even though they may contradict past ideas. One resists the Spirit when he rejects new insights in the Word because it is contrary to "what we've always thought."

We do not reject tradition as such, but must evaluate it by divine truth. One of the great privileges of the human experience is what psychologists refer to as "time-binding power." By this is meant the ability man has to reach back into history and select those things which time has proved to be of value and channel them into our time through our lives! Ours is the privilege of selecting the best from literature, from historical data, and from traditions of any heritage and channeling it into society again through our lives. Hence, to reject tradition leaves one a pauper, but to be enslaved by tradition makes one a puppet.

Many a Christian has committed the sin of resisting the Spirit in being closed to further spiritual insights. Peter, while on the house-top at Joppa, faced the question of yielding to the Spirit or resisting Him. Peter had received the Holy Spirit, yet he was imperfect in his understanding of God's will. The Lord gave him a vision in which He let down a sheet of mixed animals three times, until He broke through Peter's race prejudice, and Peter yielded to the Spirit (see Acts 10). One need meditate only a moment to see how much the spread of the gospel would have been hindered if Peter had resisted the Spirit, and rejected the new insight of truth.

The racial tensions of our day have their roots in this same human pride in one's own cultural and ethnic background. These divisions will exist in part as long as man exists, since sinful man is servant of his own pride. However, the redeeming grace of God and the redemptive mission of the church are to make all people one in Christ. In God's redemptive program there is neither Greek nor Jew, Barbarian, Scythian, bond, nor free (see Col. 3:11). The answer to racial tension is not found in force but in spiritual freedom. The church must rise to this challenge just as it did at Antioch, Philippi, and at the house of Philemon.

How often Christians have failed to follow the Spirit, and have not distinguished between their cultural practices and Christian principles, thus hindering the Spirit from leading them in some further spiritual conquest. One is guilty of resisting the Spirit when he refuses to be open to more complete understanding of the Word and will of God. Confessing our imperfection and acknowledging the Spirit's work in the "perfecting of the saints," we resist the Spirit when we are satisfied with the status quo. A spiritual leader is one who stands both outside and above the status quo and inspires persons to follow him as he follows Christ.

Rejecting the Spirit's Sanctifying Work

The Bible says, "And we all, with unveiled face, beholding the glory of the Lord, are being changed into his likeness from one degree of glory to another; for this comes from the Lord who is the Spirit" (2 Cor. 3:18). This is a significant text concerning the sanctifying work of the Spirit in the life of the believer. The Spirit reveals Christ in His Word. Numerous passages refer to the sanctification of the Spirit, meaning the way in which the Spirit works within believing hearts to conform us to the image of Christ. We are guilty of resisting the Spirit when we defend our present level of holiness as satisfactory. The Spirit works to "take every thought captive to obey Christ" (2 Cor. 10:5), and He "intercedes for us with sighs too deep for words" (Rom. 8:26). He is working to make our privileges in Christ become practical realities in daily living. We resist the Spirit when we reject His sanctifying suggestions.

Many professing Christians have never been honest with themselves or with God with respect to the sin question. Some want only enough religion to give them a false security. They are like the man who wrote to the Internal Revenue Service: "I can't sleep; my conscience is bothering me. Enclosed find a check for fifty dollars. If I still can't sleep, I'll send you the balance!" Many want God to remove their guilt but not their graft. They want His peace but not His presence.

The term "victory" is strange to the ears of many believers. Many thank God for His forgiving grace but fail to take hold of His enabling grace. Yet, the Bible says, "This is the victory that overcomes the world, our faith" (1 John 5:4). As Christians, we are engaged in a spiritual conquest. We have a known enemy—the world, the flesh, and the devil. As assurance for our victory, in Christ we have a superior power, for "he who is in you is greater than he who is in the world" (1 John 4:4).

Victory depends upon concentration of effort on the true front. In the spiritual life we must permit the Spirit to lead us into this "singleness of heart." There must be an identification with Christ that results in a crucifixion of the self, the false self that has deceived us and been untrue to God. Only when we break from the old life as definitely as death itself, can we share the new resurrection life. We can then testify with Paul, "I have been crucified with Christ; it is no longer I who live but Christ who lives in me; and the life I now live in the flesh I live by faith in the Son of God, who loved me and gave himself for me" (Gal. 2:20).

To use our God-given personality for the glory of self rather than the glory of Christ is to resist the will of the Spirit. Paul writes. ''Do you not know that your body is the temple of the Holy Spirit within you, which you have from God? You are not your own; you were bought with a price. So glorify God in your body'' (1 Cor. 6:19-20). The Spirit is working to bring our entire personality into conformity with His holiness. When we retain attitudes, actions, or appearances that are inconsistent with the mind of Christ, we are not sinning merely against a church, creed, or custom, but against the Spirit of Christ.

Since salvation is of grace, and God working redemption in us, to resist the Spirit is to sin against the only redemptive power that functions in our lives. Paul says, "Work out your own salvation with fear and trembling; for God is at work in you both to will and to work for his good pleasure" (Phil. 2:12-13). Here Paul says we are to work out life's expression that which God is working into our experience! How can we express Christ, or express truly good works, unless the Spirit of Christ is permitted to work graciously in our lives? We resist the Spirit when we oppose His way of perfecting saints. We resist Him when we offer a counterfeit perfection which measures up to some prescribed order rather than to the holiness of Christ. We resist the Spirit when we withstand His perfecting work in order to uphold our own program.

During a series of evangelistic meetings, I once visited a man who claimed to be an atheist. In the course of the conversation, he asked, "You look at me as a sinner, don't you?" I replied that all persons outside of Christ are sinners. "You count me a lost soul who needs to be saved, don't you?" he responded. After further conversation, he said, "I want to ask you a question. I boldly say there is no God and go out and live as I please. What about all those who claim to be Christians who say there is a God, and then go out and live as they please?" Obviously, he had pointed up the great sin of "practical atheism."

It must be acknowledged there is a little atheism in the heart of every man when he shoves God out of the center of his life and asserts self. To resist the Spirit is to partake of this sin! It is no small wonder that Jesus said, "If any man would come after me, let him deny himself and take up his cross daily and follow me" (Luke 9:23). In this sense we must die to live! We cannot share the full life of His sanctifying grace until we are willing to share the cross. Coming to Calvary for salvation is not the end of one's experience with the cross; it is only the beginning

We have observed that the sin of resisting the Spirit is an attitude of the heart which comes from man's basic revolt against God. It is the common sin in the unbeliever which prevents him from yielding to the regenerating work of the Holy Spirit. Many are those unbelievers in the church and out of the church, who resist the Spirit to their own damnation, never coming to know a spiritual birth through Him.

We have noted also that this sin is committed in the lives of believers, as an expression of the basic sin-tendency which revolts against the Lord. Believers need to find deliverance from the self-life, with its forms of self-satisfaction, self-defense, and self-confidence, which stand as evidence of resisting the Spirit. Only a life of true yieldedness, with a dying out to self, will result in a proper relation to the Holy Spirit.

CHAPTER 4
Quenching the Spirit

Do not quench the Spirit.
1 Thessalonians 5:19

ONE IS SAID TO BE a good conversationalist when he is a good listener. One learns most when in his exchange of ideas he is open to the ideas communicated by another. When a person is so occupied with his own ideas that he suppresses or prevents the other from communicating, he is robbing himself. This often happens in the lives of believers in the fellowship of the saints. Many worship services or private devotional periods are so outlined as to prevent the expressions of the Spirit's gifts.

When individuals are closed to advice from others, they make themselves paupers. On the other hand, there is the "Yes, yes" person who agrees with everyone and settles on no convictions of his own. These two extremes are illustrated by two battered wrecks of humanity that met on a park bench. Obviously, neither one had discovered the secret of success. One commented, "My trouble is that I'd never take advice." The other replied, "My trouble is that I took everybody's advice." In the Christian church there are too many who do not have convictions of their own, but merely say yes to the last conference speaker. Believers must go deeper than the interesting platitudes that humor them, to the inspired principles that will hold them. We need a word from the Lord that will grip the heart and guide the soul.

Paul, writing to the Thessalonian church, addresses a number of concerns to the church fellowship, in the midst of which he says, "Do not quench the Spirit." A look at the context adds meaning to this phrase. Paul is saying, "Honor and love those church leaders laboring among you, be at peace among yourselves, contribute to each other spiritually, return good for evil, rejoice continually, pray perseveringly, be thankful in every circumstance, do not quench the Spirit, do not spurn the gifts and messages of the prophets, test all things to ascertain the good, and let God sanctify your entire life." According to the context, it appears that Paul means by our text, "Do not suppress or subdue expressions of the Spirit in your fellowship."

The word "quench" literally means to "choke out," to suppress or subdue. Far too often our programs choke out the Spirit's promptings. To quench the Spirit is to choke out those inner promptings that would advance the kingdom of Christ either within us or through us. The Spirit is quenched when we refuse to yield to the revealed will of God. Paul adds, "Test everything," because not every inner impulse in the believer's life is of the divine Spirit. For example, in Acts 16 Paul had an inner urge and desire to go into Bithynia, but as he waited on God "the Spirit of Jesus did not allow them" (Acts 16:7).

On the other hand, one need only meditate a moment to discern how serious the mistake would have been if Philip had quenched the Spirit when told to go down to the road leading to Gaza, where he led the Ethiopian eunuch to Christ. Suppose Barnabas had quenched the Spirit's leading to recommend Paul to the brethren at Jerusalem, or the church leaders had promoted other plans of their own when the Holy Spirit said, "Set apart for me Barnabas and Saul for the work to which I have called them" (Acts 13:2). How often the work of Christ has been retarded because we have quenched the voice of the Spirit and substituted our own opinions.

Refusing the Spirit's Plan for Our Lives

God is personally interested in every believer. He has given various gifts to individuals that will fill a variety of needs in His church. In planning our own life and vocation, rather than searching out His will, we often quench the Spirit. First, to be in the will of God is becoming willing to do His will, although we may not know at the time what that plan is. Second, to be in His will is to seek His leading and fit our lives into it. How often believers determine their own life plan and then ask God's blessing upon it! God isn't man's servant; He is our Sovereign. We don't use God; we yield to Him. Many talented people in the churches across the land are using their talents for self rather than for Christ. If such persons would cease quenching the Spirit, and submit themselves to the will of God, the work of the kingdom could be revitalized. The believer must be willing to sacrifice his own plans for a better plan from God.

The church is the dwelling place of the Spirit and is to be directed by the Spirit. In a living, dynamic church there are always new issues to be faced, especially on the growing edge of extension. In such instances the church needs prophetic guidance. Far too often the Spirit is quenched because men are not open to His leading. Instead of meeting new situations His way, we try on "Saul's armor," which may have served him well, but has never been proved as the answer for the present crisis (see 1 Sam. 17:38-40). Due to fear of man we safeguard the status quo and quench the

Spirit. The thrilling thing about the Jerusalem conference was not that they had a conference "platform," but that they ascertained the Spirit's program (see Acts 15).

The Spirit is not only quenched with respect to the character of our service but with respect to the quality of our service. There are numerous miniature or mediocre Christians in the church. The Spirit is not satisfied with less than our best in God's service. Mediocre Christians have at some point "choked out" the voice of the Spirit. Having quenched or subdued His promptings, they became careless and indifferent about spiritual exercises.

The great Southern preacher, Robert G. Lee, speaks of mediocrity with irony, pointing out the folly of being "miniature Methodists, puny Presbyterians, bantam Baptists, pygmy Pentecostals"— and, speaking for my own denomination, I might add "midget Mennonites." This matter of being less than the best possible is illustrated in the story of a couple attending a social function at which the man sought to be the life of the party. His wife commented that she had a model husband. Upon returning home he cheeked the dictionary and found that "model" means "a small imitation of the real thing." Many church members are "small imitations" of what God really plans for them.

Lukewarm Christians are evidence of the sin of "choking out" the voice of the Spirit. No church fellowship can grow spiritually where the Spirit of God is not honored as its very life! When the lives of Christians are lukewarm and carnal, rather than dedicated and holy, it is evident that the Spirit is being quenched. Such a church is in need of a deep moving of the Spirit of God in a biblical revival. Yet such churches are often skeptical about a spiritual resurgence and are afraid of the term "revival." Since revival is the *Reviver* in action, to subdue the moving of revival is to quench or suppress the work of the Spirit. This sin leaves the church cold, empty, and spiritually dead.

Ignoring the Spirit's Gifts for Spiritual Growth

The church belongs to Christ. He is the Head, and He endows His people with those gifts necessary to succeed in His work. He speaks of these as "gifts of the Holy Spirit distributed according to his own will" (Heb. 2:4). Again He says, "To each is given the manifestation of the Spirit for the common good" (1 Cor. 12:7). And again, "All these are inspired by one and the same Spirit who apportions to each one individually as he wills" (1 Cor. 12:11). The gifts of the Spirit referred to in the Bible are direct manifestations of the Spirit working through the believer. Such manifestations can be expressed by the Spirit only in a yielded life.

We are so accustomed to organization that we fail to recognize inspiration. We revere men of the past who spoke prophetically, but we regard contemporary voices for revival as beneath our level of dignity. Dr. Vance Havner said in a Bible conference I attended, "It's a lot easier to commemorate prophets than to copy them." We often transfer a conviction from a man of vision to a committee for verification only to see it die. A committee adds power when the Spirit enlarges the conviction to grip each heart. On the other hand, a committee without conviction is so much machinery without power. It has been said that the average committee of five has one man to do the work, three to pat him on the back, and one to bring in a minority report!

From the study of the Word it appears that God's gifts are limited to His purpose, not to time. God gives His gifts according to His own will. We are to covet the best gifts for the work of the kingdom. Those gifts are best which the Spirit gives to the yielded soul, that His purpose may be accomplished. These gifts are for Christian service, and vary in lives of believers according to God's purpose for a given individual.

Gifts and service are not in themselves evidences of spirituality. The Corinthian Church had gifts, but they were carnal. On the other hand, some very spiritual Christians for some legitimate reason cannot engage in active service. Spirituality is primarily dependent upon yieldedness to the Spirit and the expression Christlike character through His abiding in us. Every believer ought to check his motive for desiring certain gifts, as he may suppress the real purpose of the Spirit in his fleshly desire for a particular gift for personal advantage.

Having recognized that humble Christians do not limit God in expressing the gifts of the Spirit, it must be noted that no one gift is expected to be seen in all true Christians. Paul makes clear that the fruit of the Spirit is to be found in all who have received Him. John adds, "He who does not love does not know God" (1 John 4:8). However, discussing the gifts of the Spirit, Paul uses a grammatical construction in the Greek that anticipates a negative answer when he asks, "Not all are workers of miracles, are they? Not all have gifts of healing, do they? Not all speak with tongues, do they?" (see 1 Cor. 12:20, 30.) The expected answer is—No. Let no one go beyond Paul in insisting that some gift is a necessary proof of the Spirit's presence, and on the other hand, let none be unfair to the message of Paul in denying the possibility of gifts.

The Spirit is often quenched by our ignoring the Spirit's ministry of giving gifts for the perfecting of the church. Paul writes, "And his gifts were that some should be apostles, some prophets, some evangelists, some pastors and teachers, to equip the saints for the work of the ministry, for building up the body of Christ, until we all attain the unity of the faith and of the knowledge of the Son of God, to mature manhood, to the measure of the stature of the fullness of Christ" (Eph. 4:11-13). Paul writes Timothy to stir up the gift that was in him through the laying on of the hands of the church leaders. The church ought to be praying that God would qualify men for various callings, such as evangelism, and then "seek out" and use those whom God qualifies. Due respect for the Spirit's work will result in men gifted for the task. Let us not suppress His work, nor work against Him by "putting a square peg in a round hole" when, had we prayed and sought His man for each task, the work would move forward under His anointing.

True spiritual leaders are prepared for their roles by the anointing of the Spirit. Leaders are not made merely by use of a ballot. The church will profit only by spiritual leadership, not by leadership of the majority vote. Leadership in the church of Christ is a spiritual matter, as anointed men discern the mind of Christ. To conform to the Word of God, we should only follow religious leaders if they prove themselves worthy to lead. A church will die if it emphasizes conformity to authorities within the church to the exclusion of originality that the Spirit's anointing would produce through various individuals.

Suppressing the Spirit's Insights

The Spirit has come to guide us into all truth. As we study the Bible, the Spirit brings to bear upon our lives new insights that will advance our spiritual growth. We are commanded to grow in grace. Many believers have a prolonged spiritual infancy because they have long quenched the Spirit in suppressing His voice. The old saying applies here, "None is so blind as he who will not see." The sin of suppressing the Spirit's insights rather than surrendering to them has robbed many a professing Christian of joy in the Lord. Some Christians after ten or twenty years have less joy and enthusiasm than at the time of their conversion. There are many church members whom God has long sought to lead into His fullness, who are habitually quenching the Spirit and thus robbing themselves of the fruitfulness of the abundant life.

Quenching the Spirit is a sin marked by complacency, indifference, and being satisfied with the status quo. The Bible refers to this sin as self-righteousness, counting oneself as good enough in his present state. Such persons are closed to further revelation of God's purpose in their lives. They defend their present limitation like the fanatic "who can't change his opinion and will not change the subject." This sin is evidence of a pathetically inadequate concept of the spiritual life. Such persons are not looking at Jesus and saying with Paul, "That I may know him and the power of his resurrection, and may share his sufferings" (Phil. 3:10), but rather measure themselves by an inadequate carnal standard.

The result of quenching the Spirit is spiritual apostasy. Such persons are described by Paul as "lovers of self ... lovers of pleasures rather than lovers of God, holding the form of religion, but denying the power of it" (2 Tim. 3:2, 4-5). The effect of this sin within one's self is a dying-out spiritually. A literal translation from the Greek of Paul's words in Romans 8:6 reads, "To be carnally minded leads down to death," and again in 8:13, "If you live after the flesh, you are about to die." In contrast, the believer is called to walk in the Spirit.

These are days of much religion but little righteousness. There is much talk about revival but little willingness to pay the price.

Church membership may be high, but religion without morality is not enough. The Bible foretells apostasy in the church in the last days. The church of the present time is in this apostasy and has failed to recognize it. Today's church is known by lukewarmness rather than by love aflame. We have borrowed the world's gimmicks and have often substituted organization for His anointing. We need to beware of a *synthetic* Pentecost. We need a fresh moving of God's Spirit to break through the coldness and indifference of our time. Once again the gospel "plow" must be placed into the soil of the human heart to "break up your fallow ground" (Hosea 10:12). We have become idolaters in being "lovers of pleasure rather than lovers of God" (2 Tim. 3:4). We have the forms of godliness but lack the fellowship. We have the doctrine but lack the devotion. Only as we open our lives to His Spirit will He lead us in the conquest of His holiness.

In concluding this study on quenching the Spirit, it is significant to see how many believers fail to appropriate the promise of God in Christ. Paul says that all things are ours in Christ, yet it is up to the believer to hearken to the Spirit in possessing our possessions. In Joshua 1:2-3, there is a unique illustration of this privilege and of man's failure. God told Joshua, "Arise, go over this Jordan, you and all this people, into the land which I am giving to them, to the people of Israel. Every place that the sole of your foot will tread upon I have given to you, as I promised to Moses." Here God said "I have given it to you"; then later He says, "Whatever you claim, I have given you." God has given us promises, but they become our possession only as we follow the Spirit in claiming them.

Studying the conquest of Canaan, we discover that the people of Israel made three outstanding mistakes in not possessing all their possessions. These mistakes involved the Gibeonites, the Jebusites, and the Canaanites or Philistines; and they were mistakes of the *mind*, the *heart*, and the *flesh*.

The first mistake was that of the mind, in which Joshua failed to pray concerning a league with the strangers and followed his own reasoning, only to find that he had made a league with people God intended to remove from the land. How often by *self-confidence* we make a league with things in our lives that the Spirit of God intended to root out!

Second, we find the sin of *self-justification*, in that Israel permitted the Jebusites to dwell in the heart of the land, the area destined to be the capital, and because of this mistake they suffered by the hand of these giants. Many times professing Christians have failed to bring the heart of their life under subjection to Christ, and suffer defeat after defeat. The Spirit would make the very heart of one's life the throne of Christ, but too often the heart does not yield to His lordship until long after it might have benefited from this privilege in Christ.

Third, we find the sin of *self-satisfaction*, a sin of the flesh in being satisfied with less than God's best. The people were told to bring all Canaan under their possession, and leave no room for the enemies of Jehovah. However, after they had brought a percentage of the land under their control, and had found satisfaction for their immediate needs, they discontinued the warfare, with many Philistines yet in the land. Throughout the history of Israel these remaining Philistines were a source of problems. From them the Israelites learned pagan practices and adopted various forms of idolatry.

As a result of Israel's sin they lost God's power for victory and were overrun by the Philistines. Defeated, they would cry to God for help, overcome the Philistines, then yielding to sin again would repeat the cycle over and over. Many Christians have a pattern of defeat, repentance, and joy—all because they do not break entirely with sin. The Bible says. "Put on the Lord Jesus Christ, and make no provision for the flesh" (Rom. 13:14).

The Spirit's work is to bring the believer's life into complete acceptance of the will of Christ. The believer is called of God to be a temple of the Holy Spirit. Once the Shekinah glory rested over the tabernacle, but from the little flames of glory at Pentecost until the present the Spirit rests in His Shekinah glory upon the individual believer. Redeemed by the blood, we are His purchased possession, called to yield to Him.

The nature of this sin of quenching the Spirit is a lack of yieldedness. Paul writes of our salvation, "Do you not know that your body is a temple of the Holy Spirit within you which you have of God? You are not your own; you were bought with a price. So glorify God in your body" (Cor. 6:19-20). It follows that the cure for this sin is willing obedience. The Bible says, "If we live by the Spirit, let us also walk by the Spirit" (Gal. 5:25). One who walks in the Spirit is sensitive to the voice of the Spirit. As we seek to do His will, the message of His Word becomes alive in our souls. The Lord says, "If any man's will is to do his will, he shall know whether the teaching is from God" (John 7:17). God will speak clearly to the soul who wants to hear!

Come, Holy Spirit, heavenly Dove,
With all Thy quickening powers
Kindle a flame of sacred love
In these cold hearts of ours.

In vain we tune our formal songs,
In vain we strive to rise;

Hosannas languish on our tongues,
And our devotion dies.

Dear Lord, and shall we ever live
At this poor dying rate?
Our love so faint, so cold to Thee,
And Thine to us so great!

Come, Holy Spirit, heavenly Dove,
With all Thy quickening powers;
Come, shed abroad a Savior's love,
And that shall kindle ours.

— Isaac Watts

CHAPTER 5

Grieving the Spirit

And do not grieve the Holy Spirit of God, in whom you were sealed for the day of redemption.
Ephesians 4:30

GOD'S PROGRAM IN THE WORLD is to make saints out of sinners. As the Spirit moves upon man, he is brought to a personal faith in the finished work of Calvary. In this experience, God in forgiving grace wraps His arms of love around us in true acceptance. The effect of the cross within the believer's life is a practical cleansing from the guilt and power of sin.

Cleansing is not a matter of God's overlooking the sin within the sinner's life, but rather of dealing with it. Cleansing is God's act of separating the sin from the sinner. In the numerous cleansing tasks of a household, the dirt is not covered over, but rather separated from that which it has made dirty. So God through the provision of the cross separates the believing heart from the old practices of sin. Paul said, "Far be it from me to glory except in the cross of our Lord Jesus Christ, by which the world has been crucified to me, and I to the world" (Gal. 6:14).

Many believers have taken the problem of sin too lightly. It is truly a marvel of God's grace that when He forgives, He does so knowing that He'll need to forgive again, and again, and again.

However, grace carries more benefit than forgiveness; it creates a new life. Too often believers hold a narrow view of grace and miss its transforming function. The Bible says, "sin will have no dominion over you, since you are not under law but under grace" (Rom. 6:14).

The greatest hindrance to the testimony of the church is that believers deny the validity of grace for victory, and thereby bring reproach upon the gospel by living sub-Christian lives. Such persons are even adept in finding ways of discovering how to get by with their sin. They are like the man who went to confessional and first of all reached over and picked the priest's pocket, and stole his watch. In the course of the confession, he said, "I've stolen a watch." The priest replied, "Take it back." The man said, "Here, you take it," but the priest answered, "No, give it back to the man you stole it from." The man replied, "I've offered it to him and he won't take it." Whereupon the priest answered, "Then you may keep it!" No person can know the joy of God's forgiveness without dealing honestly with his sin.

Having cleansed believers and made them His own, the Lord has given the Holy Spirit to those who obey Him (see Acts 5:32). The presence of the Spirit seals us into a fellowship of holiness in Christ. The Spirit is at work within the believing heart "to equip the saints for the work of ministry" (Eph. 4:12). It is the Christian's responsibility to understand and yield to this work. The Spirit's concern over His own possession is expressed in James 4:5 (Amplified N.T.): "Do you suppose that the Scripture is speaking to no purpose that says, the Spirit whom He has caused to dwell in us yearns over us—and He yearns for the Spirit—with a jealous love?" He is spiritual who is sensitive to the voice and purpose of the Spirit and obeys Him. Every known sin is committed by voluntary choice.

In the practice of known sin the believer is rejecting the will of the Spirit.

In Romans 8:13, Paul points up the danger of a believer's living after the flesh in the words, "If you live according to the flesh you will die," or literally from the Greek, "You are on the way to die." Of this sin, René Pache says: "Those who knowingly and willingly continue to grieve the Spirit indefinitely by refusing to be sanctified will ultimately reach perdition. God's Word speaks plainly: "Follow after ... sanctification without which no man shall see the Lord" (Heb. 12:14). Therefore let us awake and cry unto God, beseeching Him to deliver us from this body of death. This He will surely do if we are sincere, for He desires to give us the victory."[1]

It is of such sin in the life of the believer that Paul writes to the Ephesians, "Do not grieve the Holy Spirit of God." The Greek expresses it, "Stop grieving the Spirit," or bring to an end those practices that grieve the Spirit. This statement lies in a section of Paul's epistle (4:26-32) in which he calls attention to the contrast between the old nature and the new nature. The old nature he identifies with the "former manner of life" (verse 22), with the "body of flesh" (Col. 2:11), and elsewhere as the reign of sin (Rom. 6:12). In Romans 6:6 Paul distinguishes between the old self and sin tendency, clearly stating that the old nature is crucified, so that the "body of sin" (KJV) might be destroyed, or literally, "devitalized." In Colossians 3, Paul makes this distinction clear by saying, "Ye have put off the old man.... Now ... also put off all these" (verses 8, 9 KJV). Paul's concern is that in the life of one who has had a death experience to the old nature and is called to a life of holiness, there should be no permission for the sin tendency to express itself.

It becomes clear in the study of this passage that the Spirit is grieved because of the presence of sin. The Spirit dwells within the believer to perfect holiness, and known sin comes into that life only by a voluntary choice. This choice is made between the pleasure of sin and the perfection of Christ. The serious thing is not the size of the sin, but the fact that when one deliberately chooses some sin over against the full fellowship of Christ, one is demonstrating his preference between the two. The Spirit is grieved by the presence of sin, but He is even more grieved because an individual has chosen the pleasure of sin rather than the pursuit of God!

The Sin of Self-Will Grieves the Spirit

The believer is to have died to the self-life by enthroning Jesus Christ as the center of his life. It is true both theologically and psychologically that the only deliverance from a self-centered life is to have a new center! It is the work of the Holy Spirit to make Christ real as the new center of the believer's life. The rise of self-will is thus an act of treason against the new Ruler. It is an attempt at replacing Christ with self. When a believer drags over into the new life things that were characteristic of his old life, he is defying the new Master! The lordship of Christ dare not be an *impersonal doctrine*; it is to be a *personal discipline*. All of life is to be brought under His lordship.

In the context of our reference to grieving the Spirit, Paul speaks of "putting away falsehood ... we are members one of another. Be angry but do not sin ... give no opportunity to the devil" (Eph. 4:25-27). Paul is saying, "Let the believer be honest, rather than dishonest in an attempt to advance some selfish purpose. Let the believer have a righteous indignation against sin, but let him never have anger against a person in a way that violates his call to love." We must always separate the issue from the personality. Let the believer give no place to the adversary in opposing the work of the Spirit in sanctifying the church. As believers, we are a part of the church, and we give up our own individualism for the sake of the larger program of His kingdom.

We need to discover that we are sinners not so much for what we have done as for what we are. It is true not only that we have sinned but that we are sinful. The sin problem is not answered by disciplining the external conduct but by dealing with the internal control. Once the self-life has been dealt with through the cross and Christ is Ruler of the life through His Spirit, the entire life takes on new motivation and new meaning. This new life in Christ becomes nonconformed to the former life in sin.

We were leading selfish lives when we were outside of Christ and in sin. Now, in Christ, under new control, the Spirit is grieved when we seek to assert self again. Paul asks the Galatians, "Are you so foolish? Having begun with the Spirit, are you now ending with the flesh?" (Gal. 3:3). Many Christians grieve the Spirit in that after they have asked God for salvation they revert to confidence in the flesh. They seek to live the Christian life by the efforts of the flesh, even calling the latter obedience! True obedience is yieldedness to the lordship of Christ and His Spirit.

Sins of Commission Grieve the Spirit

Sins of commission are overt acts contrary to the will of Christ. The sin of self-will is the basic sin, for God defines sin in the words, "We have turned every one to his own way" (Isa. 53:6). However, sin not only has a cause; it has an effect. It has both an exponent and an expression. Sinful expressions in the lives of believers become the greatest hindrances to the testimony of the gospel and the church. The sinner looks at the Christian with the question, "How can you tell me that Christ will save me from sin when He hasn't delivered you from yours?" Many a professing Christian has no testimony because he retains some pet sin and grieves the Spirit.

We are told to "lay aside every weight and sin which clings so closely" (Heb. 12:1). Many professing Christians hinder God's work and their witness by not dealing with besetting sin. One of the hindrances to revival is that ninety percent of the Christian church doesn't expect to change! In a community-wide evangelistic crusade which I was privileged to conduct, one of those responding was a man some fifty years old. Confessing that be had been bound by a habit almost forty years, he told how when he invited some employees to church, he overheard one of them comment, "How can he tell us that Christ will deliver us from sin when he is still bound?"

It is wise to be honest about one's weakest point and concentrate faith to build strength there. Satan knows best where to make his advances. To our shame we try to cover our weakness rather than correct it. Even as you read this, God calls you to deal with your besetting sin. Do you recognize it? It is the one you are thinking of right now! It is the one you don't want to call sin, that you have excuses for, that occupies your first attention, that you defend most ardently, and that you don't want to give up. Face it. You hold on to a sin only because you love that sin more than you love the Savior!

Sins of commission may be sins of attitude, action, or of appearance. Paul speaks of sins of *attitude* in the words, "Let all bitterness and wrath and anger and clamor and slander be put away from you, with all malice" (Eph. 4:31). Attitudes of indifference, ill will, uncharitable criticism, envy, haughtiness, holier-than-thouness all grieve the Spirit. These are sins against the unity of the Spirit and the bond of peace. Such is the prevalent sin of egotism. As someone has said, "A bore is a person who keeps talking of himself when you'd like to be talking of yourself."

In our text Paul refers to sins of *action* in the words, "Let the thief no longer steal.... Let no evil talk come out of your mouths.... But fornication and all impurity or covetousness must not even be named among you as is fitting among saints. Let there be no filthiness, nor silly talk, nor levity, which are not fitting; but instead let there be thanksgiving" (Eph. 4:28-29, 5:3-4). In these verses Paul gives specific identification to sins that grieve the Spirit.

There are also sins in the area of *appearance* which Paul refers to elsewhere. In 1 Thessalonians 5:22 Paul says, "Abstain from every form of evil." Again he refers to the sin of immodesty and of vain outward adornment which calls attention to the flesh rather than to spiritual realities (1 Tim. 2:9-10). Vain display for selfish and sexual attraction grieves the Spirit, while the true adornment of developing a Christlike character and personality is blessed of God. The former is easy, in adding external tinsel, while the latter is the difficult challenge of developing true Christian character.

The behavior of the believer's life must be tested before the criteria of the mind of Christ. No single passage in the Bible attempts to outline a catalog of sins that will be specific in every culture and time. Rather, the Spirit calls us to evaluate behavior patterns by the divine pattern, Jesus Christ. The believer need only recognize the Holy Spirit and allow Him to indicate whether a thing is Christlike. How much stronger the church would be if believers were all taught to consult with the Spirit over His Book rather than simply be handed a list of rules. A "prefab" Christian doesn't have the privilege of enjoying the Spirit's direction in building a superstructure of godliness.

Sins of Omission Grieve the Spirit

It is significant that in the ministry of Christ some of the sins of which He was most severe in His indictment were sins of omission rather than of commission. To the religious leaders He said, "These you ought to have done, without neglecting the others" (Matt. 23:23). Again the Bible says, "whoever knows what is right to do and fails to do it, for him it is sin" (James 4:17). Faith is a positive element. Belief implies commitment. The Christian faith is a positive following of Christ in a new life. We are told to "strive for ... holiness without which no one will see the Lord" (Heb. 12:14). Sins of omission therefore come under the indictment of "unbelief." The Epistle to the Hebrews exposes the seriousness of unbelief in using Israel as an illustration. By her sin of omission, of not going in to possess the land, Israel missed God's blessed provisions because of unbelief. Unbelief, or disbelief, is to refuse light, and to be satisfied with a way of life beneath what is understood.

Sins of omission are no doubt some of the most common in Christian experience. It is so easy to be careless or slothful about spiritual disciplines.

a. To neglect meditation on God's Word and prayer is a sin of omission which grieves the Spirit. His work of transforming the life is retarded in proportion to the way the individual neglects the Word. Jesus emphasized the place of the Word in sanctification when He said, "Sanctify them in the truth; thy word is truth" (John 17:17).

b. Failure to tithe and practice Christian stewardship is a sin of omission. Jesus gave His endorsement of the tithe when He said, "These you ought to have done" (Matt. 23:23). The Spirit is grieved by our materialistic attitudes which hinder the program of missions and evangelism.

c. Love is a positive element, outgoing by its very nature, enriching friends in Christ and winning enemies to Christ. To fail to cultivate and express love toward our fellowman is a sin of omission. In the context of our theme, Paul says, "Be kind to one another, tenderhearted, forgiving one another, as God in Christ forgave you" (Eph. 4:32). Since this is a positive command, to neglect the expression of love and kindness, which is really a fruit or expression of the Spirit, is to be guilty of a sin of omission.

d. It must also be added that one of the most common sins of omission is a failure to witness for Christ. The New Testament pattern is for every believer to be a witness. Evangelism is not to be thought of as the work of a particular man or the oratory of an evangelist. It is rather the work of the body, the church. Only as every member is a witness can the church promote the kingdom according to the will of Christ. This sin of omission is one confronting all of us. God says, "If ... you do not speak to warn the wicked to turn from his way, that wicked man shall die in his iniquity, but his blood I will require at your hand" (Ezek. 33:8).

The Spirit is grieved when we permit known sin in our lives. This is not a matter concerning unknown sin, since in the life of the true Christian, when the Spirit reveals unknown sin, he is instantly ready to confess that which is made known. The problem for most believers is in living beneath their understanding of God's will and thus grieving the Spirit.

He is called the Spirit of holiness, and we grieve Him by unholy thoughts and sinful lusts, by selfishness, and by fraternizing with the world. He is called the Spirit of truth, and we grieve Him by rationalization and by following our own opinions.

He is called the Spirit of power, and we grieve Him by suffering defeat through ignoring His power. He is called the Spirit of faith, and we grieve Him by permitting doubts rather than searching the truth. He is called the Spirit of love, and we grieve Him by lack of love, both toward fellow believers and toward enemies who need salvation.

He is called the Spirit of unity, and we grieve Him by division and partiality. He is the Spirit at work, and we grieve Him by indifference to God's program of evangelism. Let us stop grieving the Spirit and obey Him consistently.

Of the seriousness of this sin, René Pache writes:

> If God respects our liberty, as soon as we elect to sin rather than obey His will, He suspends His activity within bur hearts and breaks His communion with us. From then onward the power of the Spirit is no longer made manifest through us; we stand powerless before the tempter and suffer one defeat after another. Realizing such a weakness in their spiritual life and witness, many cry out to God, praying at length while despairingly fighting for victory, for they imagine that the Savior has no wish to help or is withholding His assistance for a while. But the truth is that the obstacle lies in themselves. So long as the Spirit is grieved, He will take no step toward their deliverance.[2]

A concluding observation from Joshua 7 will point up the seriousness of this sin for us. In the conquest of Jericho, God's presence had been manifest in a miraculous way, bringing victory to

Israel. God led Israel into Canaan by the miracle of parting Jordan's waters for them to march across, illustrating for that generation, as He had for their fathers at the Red Sea, that men move from the bondage of sin into the fellowship of God only by a miracle of grace. In the conquest of Jericho it was alone by God's power and presence that Israel was victorious, illustrated in the place given to the ark as a symbol of God's presence.

Following the conquest of Jericho, Joshua sent men against Ai; however, they were defeated! The ark, was present as a symbol of God's presence, but God did not express His power. As Joshua prostrated himself before the Lord in prayer, God said; "Arise, why have you thus fallen upon your face? Israel has sinned; they have transgressed my covenant which I commanded them; they have taken some of the devoted things; they have stolen, and lied, and put them among their own stuff. Therefore the people of Israel cannot stand before their enemies; they turn their backs before their enemies ... I will be with you no more, unless you destroy the devoted things from among you" (Josh. 7:10-12).

Even though God was present, He refused to express His power because of man's sin. God had said that all the treasures taken from Jericho, the first city, belonged to Him. In further conquests the treasures could be used by Israel. Thus the things taken from Jericho were "devoted" to the Lord but when Achan took the devoted things to himself, it became a curse to him! As a result, God's power would not function in the face of disobedience. So in the Christian life, God asks that the first loyalty be given to Him; then the rest of life can be enjoyed by the individual in the light of the basic commitment.

When men take back that first loyalty, the devoted thing, and use it for self, the Spirit is grieved and God's power is hindered.

The person may have had a unique experience with God; however, even though God may be present, He withholds His power because of the sin. God cannot wisely bless Christian lives or Christian workers where there is known sin, for in doing so He is placing His stamp of approval upon their lives while they yet remain in that sin. The size of the sin, in man's judgment, may not be very large. However, the seriousness of it does not consist in the size but in the choice. Achan lost his relation with God for a small thing—six hundred and twenty dollars and an overcoat. Yet the choice demonstrated that he loved his sin more than he loved God.

The Christian's challenge is to give one's self to prayer, spiritual discernment, and obedience, lest the Spirit be grieved by sin. The answer to this sin problem is entire consecration.

When D. L. Moody was visiting England to discover a fuller answer to his spiritual hunger, he heard Henry Varley say, "The world has yet to see what God will do with a man who is fully and wholly consecrated to Him." Mr. Moody later testified that he thought "Varley said 'a man.' He didn't say a great or learned man, not a rich or a wise man, nor an eloquent man, or a smart man, but simply—a man!" Moody decided, "I am a man, and it lies within the man himself whether he will or will not make that entire and full consecration. By the grace of God, I will be that man."

History has revealed the value of such consecration under God's anointing. Let us meet the same challenge, and pray with the hymn writer:

Lord, I am fondly, earnestly longing
Into Thy holy likeness to grow;
Thirsting for more and deeper communion,
Yearning Thy love more fully to know.

Dead to the world would I be, O Father!
Dead unto sin, alive unto Thee;
Crucify all the earthly within me,
Emptied of sin and self may I be.

I would be Thine, and serve Thee forever,
Filled with Thy Spirit, lost in Thy love;
Come to my heart, Lord, come with anointing,
Showers of grace send down from above.

Refrain:
Open the wells of grace and salvation,
Pour the rich streams deep into my heart;
Cleanse and refine my thought and affection,
Seal me and make me pure as Thou art.

— E. A. Hoffman

CHAPTER 6

Lying to the Spirit

But Peter said, "Ananias, why has Satan filled your heart to lie to the Holy Spirit, and to keep back part of the proceeds of the land?.... You have not lied to men but to God."
Acts 5:3-4

ONE OF LIFE'S GREATEST VIRTUES is honesty, honesty with one's self and with God. One of man's greatest sins, both psychologically and spiritually, is the sin of dishonesty. When man lies to himself, he sins against the conscience which would call him to do what he understands to be right. Such is the sin of one who tells himself he can sin and get by. Such was the sin of Balaam, who, knowing what God had said, told his own conscience, "I will see what God will tell me more!" (Num. 22:19, free translation.) There is the deeper aspect of this sin, in that man not only lies to himself, but since the Spirit of God is at work within his soul, he may commit the sin of lying to the Spirit!

Dishonesty is one of the most subtle sins in human experience. It prevents a man from meeting the challenges of life in a realistic attitude, and prevents the soul from admitting its spiritual need of regeneration. Many persons live as though success comes only by pulling strings to secure one's goal. The story is told of two brothers operating a feed mill in a rural area. Ono attended revival meetings at a community church and was converted. He immediately witnessed to his brother about his need of conversion. Finally the brother replied, "I'd like to join the church, but now that you've joined, somebody in this business must weigh in the wheat." This rather common sin can encroach upon a person's spiritual experience until he is not honest with God.

As we study the account of the sin of Ananias and Sapphira, we want to discover the essence of their sin. We will also note the effect and seriousness of this sin on man's spiritual experience. Because their sin resulted in immediate death, we are inclined to feel that the sin was something very unusual; however, this is not the case. This sin is a common one within the church of our time and carries with it a sentence of spiritual death. In the beginning days of the church, God dealt with this sin in a drastic way as a lesson that members of the true church of Christ are called to transparent honesty before the Lord. God gave one dramatic illustration in their death that should illustrate for all time the seriousness of this sin.

The setting of the story is significant. The church began at the season of Pentecost, when people were in Jerusalem from many parts of the world. Such a setting was in God's plan for the beginning of the church. Christianity spread into all the world as these people returned to their homes with a new faith. On the day of Pentecost itself, three thousand souls were saved and brought into the fellowship of believers. Already there had been at least five hundred believers who had been together with the Lord before His ascension (see 1 Cor. 15:6). Now, either in one invitation following Peter's sermon or by each of the five hundred bringing six more, three thousand believers were added to the church.

Not many days later the record says five thousand more came into the fellowship of the redeemed. A bit of imagination can soon help us understand what a task rested upon the leaders of the church with eight thousand new converts in less than two weeks! No doubt many of these converts were tourists who were visiting from other parts of the world. Since this gospel was new to them, likely many stayed around to become better informed in their recently received faith. Thus the local church faced the challenge of sharing financially with the visiting believers.

There is no necessary reason to assume that the church at Jerusalem established a community-of-goods association. As further evidence, one does not find a community-of-goods pattern carried into the establishment of new churches, which would logically have followed as they proclaimed that which they had learned in Jerusalem. Rather, it appears that the unselfish nature of Christianity was expressed as the Spirit of God moved upon property-holding believers to help the church. Many sold property and gave the money to help feed the believers from a distance, until they returned to their homes with an understanding of the gospel.

In this kind of setting, there was joyous enthusiasm among those who had been praying that God would open the way for them to remain longer. Money donated by such believers as Barnabas made this possible. The account suggests that these donations were voluntary, not commanded by the leaders of the church. Hence, Ananias and Sapphire were not required to sell their property, nor to give all the proceeds if they did sell. They were free to do what they felt best, and to make whatever donation they chose. However, they were responsible before God to be honest in whatever they did.

The Nature of the Sin

What was the nature of the sin of Ananias and Sapphire? The

account makes clear that the sin was tremendously serious in the eyes of God. Their sin was simply in pretending a greater spirituality than they actually possessed. It was the sin of giving a false impression. They pretended that all was on the altar for God when actually it wasn't.

As Ananias and Sapphira heard the commendation for the unselfishness of Barnabas, who apparently had property in Cyprus, and who sold his property and gave the proceeds to the church, they were motivated to make a similar donation and to share in the glory. However, as they talked it over, they decided to give only part of the money to the church and keep back the rest for themselves. This was their privilege, and had they told Peter they were giving only part of it, all would have been clear. But out of their desire for commendation by the church for giving all to the Lord, they were dishonest. They lied to the Holy Spirit by giving a false impression, by seeking recognition for a devotion that was only a sham.

As Peter exposed Ananias's sin, he didn't say, "You have lied to the church," but "You have lied to the Holy Spirit." The church is "a dwelling place of God in the Spirit" (Eph. 2:22). To sin against the standards of the Bible is not to sin against some church, but it is to sin against the Holy Spirit! As Peter goes further in his analysis, he says, "You have not lied to men but to God." Thus Peter not only confirms the relation of the church to God, but he identifies the Holy Spirit as God! The Bible speaks of the Godhead as one unity, with three personalities, Father, Son, and Holy Spirit. The Holy Spirit is God's executive or agent in the world today. This is the age of the Holy Spirit. We cannot deal with God apart from the Holy Spirit. Since the Spirit's work is to take out of the world a people for His name (see Acts 15:14), and to present to the Lord a sanctified church, to sin against the church is to sin against the

Holy Spirit.

The nature of this sin is thus to profess a devotion to Christ which we know isn't true. It is giving the impression that everything is yielded to Christ, when we know better. It is to claim that one's life is committed to Christ, but to ignore the full meaning of Paul's call to "present your bodies as a living sacrifice, holy and acceptable to God" (Rom. 12:1). It to share in the Lord's Supper as testimony that Jesus is Lord of one's life, and yet not be surrendered to Him. It is to claim to be consecrated to Him and yet refrain from giving even the tithe. It is to claim to he committed to the "all things" and then live at terms with the world rather than accept the tension of the cross. It is to claim to have given up all for the service of Christ and at the same time be quite careful to gather security for self.

As in the case of Ananias and Sapphire, it may be that the deed involved would be legitimate if the person would be honest about it, but the false impression brings condemnation. Spiritual health and vitality depend upon transparent honesty before God's searching holiness.

The church has always had to deal with unconsecrated Christians. Trouble within the church has always done more harm than trials from without. Dr. Vance Havner says, "The church is never harmed half so much by woodpeckers on the outside as by termites on the inside." The average church is plagued with an over-abundance of bench warmers—people who haven't discovered the joy of sharing the divine purpose. The work of the church will progress only as Christians are sincere in their experience, enthusiasm, and expression of faith.

One of the deadening things in Christianity today is the number of people who profess to be yielded to Christ but live for self. People lie to the Holy Spirit when they sing, "All for Jesus I surrender," and know in their hearts that they haven't yielded. Often people have lied in singing, "My Jesus I love Thee, I know Thou art mine; for Thee all the follies of sin I resign," while at the same time they are so in love with self that they follow sin rather than renounce it. The greatest heresy of our time is the idea that a person can accept Jesus as Savior without submitting to Him as Lord!

The Seriousness of the Sin

The fact that God took the lives of Ananias and Sapphira is an indication of the seriousness of this sin. Here is a lesson for all "spiritual liars" which dare not be ignored. We seem to take sin so lightly. A half-truth is justified by many a person. In the shoes of Ananias many would no doubt have justified themselves. When Peter asked; "Tell me whether you sold the land for so much?" the half-truth would be, "Yes, for so much," not adding, "and for so much more!" A "mental reservation" doesn't alter the seriousness of a lie. Dishonesty is the intent to deceive, and the so-called "white lie" is still a lie. Sin is sin, no matter how intelligently we may rationalize. Anything inferior to the holiness of Christ is sin.

Lying to the Holy Ghost is serious because it cuts off the purpose of His work within one's heart. He is present in the believer's experience, and to lie to Him about behavior is to sin against the very nature and purpose of His work. As in a counseling situation, when the counselee is dishonest, the counselor is limited in leading the person to an honest evaluation of his problem and its answer. The divine Counselor, or Comforter, who understands our revolting nature and God's redemptive work, is thwarted in His purpose of perfecting the believer in Christ when such a one is dishonest with Him.

Our lives are an open book before God. The Bible says, "Thou discernest my thoughts from afar" (Ps. 139:2), and again that God "judges the secrets of men" (Rom. 2:16). We have the privilege of being honest before God voluntarily or being exposed by God involuntarily. The old adage is true, psychologically and spiritually, that an honest confession is good for the soul.

Such a sin is serious because it is conscious and willful. One who lies to the Holy Ghost is deliberately defending his sinful act or position. There is a vast difference between sin in which one is "overtaken in a fault" (Gal. 6:1 KJV) and premeditated sin. The sin of lying to the Holy Spirit is a deliberate act of self-defense and also self-justification before His call to holiness. Such sin is an expression of men's basic sin problem, that of revolting against God.

One cannot claim to walk in the Spirit and at the same time be living for self. One cannot have God and sin, too. It is either the way of self or the way of the Spirit, for the two are at opposite poles. Lying to the Spirit is an attempt to maintain face without maintaining faith. It is an effort to pretend spirituality without being possessed by the Spirit. One lies to the Spirit when he consents that Christ is Lord but does not submit to Him as Lord.

The Effect of the Sin

Lying to the Spirit brought about the death of Ananias and Sapphira. The effect of sin is always death. The Bible says, "The wages of sin is death" (Rom. 6:23). In this case God's judgment was immediate, as a lesson to the church. God is not obligated to repeat such immediate judgments as a lesson, for the Scripture is given for our instruction. However, it would be unfair to the meaning of the account and to the justice of God if we ignored the striking lesson of the effect of this sin.

The Christian life is a relationship with Christ as Lord. One is born again, or made alive spiritually, through the work of the Holy Spirit. This new birth brings a spiritual reality into our lives, which is given life by the presence of the Holy Spirit. However, the new birth is a means to an end and not an end in itself. The born-again believer is saved, and just as saved at that moment as he ever will be; however, he is not as sanctified or mature as he ever will be!

This new babe in Christ is to grow spiritually, and spiritual growth is of God's grace through the work of the indwelling Spirit. To sin against the Spirit, to lie to Him, is to sin against the only power that seals one into fellowship with Christ and that energizes one in spiritual growth. Just as in natural life, the moment a child is born he begins to die, yet he lives because life overcomes the death influence. So in the life of the new born Christian there is always the sin potential, working death, which needs to be counteracted by the life of the Spirit. We have no life of our own as believers, but live because of our position in Christ.

The question follows, Can a born-again Christian lie spiritually? It is said, "Once one is born he cannot be unborn." However, this isn't the right figure of speech. One who is born can die! Paul writes to spiritual people in Romans 8:13, saying, "If you live according to the flesh, you will die." One immediately asks, "Is there no security for the believer?" Yes, indeed, but it is a security in Christ, not in sin. Jesus said that as we abide in Him, we abide in the Father's hand and "no one is able to snatch them out of the Father's hand" (John 10:20). The security of the Christian is stated in the words, "My sheep hear my voice, and I know them, and they follow me" (John 10:27). Without controversy, let it be acknowledged that one can have genuine assurance of salvation, of having been born again and of security in Christ, without subscribing |o the view of an unconditional eternal security which tends to antinomianism.

The effect of this sin is thus a death influence in the life of the believer. Since the new birth is the beginning of spiritual life, and a spiritual relationship, we dare not sin against it. Since God expects our freedom of the will by His own sovereign decree, we prove the validity of our faith in the free and voluntary confession of Christ as Lord. This is not some single momentous experience alone, but is a reconciliation which determines our destiny through a dynamic spiritual relationship. To sin against the Holy Spirit is to sin against this relationship. Cutting off the source of life, we become spiritually sick as the death influence continues to function. Such a backslider is by choice committing spiritual suicide.

God's purpose for every believer is obedience to His will. We are called to walk in the Spirit. Paul outlines God's purpose in the following Words: "There is therefore now no condemnation for those who are in Christ Jesus. For the law of the Spirit of life in Christ Jesus has set me free from the law of sin and death.... In order that the just requirement of the law might be fulfilled in us, who walk not according to the flesh but according to the Spirit.... Anyone who does not have the Spirit of Christ does not belong to him..... For all who are led by the Spirit of God are the sons of God" (Rom. 8:1, 2, 4, 9, 14).

Let all of us respond in dedication to Him and walk in the Spirit. In answer to this call, let each be honest with himself and with God. Abiding in Christ, we experience the security of faith in a God who saves, seals, and keeps. To place security on a mere past response rather than a momentous relationship is to rob faith of its transcendent quality and let the church sink into the mire of indifference.

The answer to this problem in the church today is found in genuine revival. As someone has said, "When the temperature is high enough, it will kill the germs." We need the kind of revival that results in confession or cleavage, experience or expulsion, sanctification or separation. When God cleansed the church of its deceit, it surged ahead with new dynamic. When your life is transparently honest before God, it will express the transforming holiness of God.

Holy Ghost, with light divine,
Shine upon this heart of mine;
Chase the shades of night away,
Turn my darkness into day.

Holy Ghost, with pow'r divine,
Cleanse this guilty heart of mine;
Long hath sin, without control,
Held dominion o'er my soul.

Holy Ghost, with joy divine,
Cheer this saddened heart of mine;
Bid my many woes depart;
Heal my wounded, bleeding heart.

Holy Spirit, all divine.
Dwell within this heart of mine;
Cast down ev'ry idol throne;
Reign supreme, and reign alone.
— Andrew Reed

CHAPTER 7

Tempting the Spirit

"How is it that you hove agreed together to tempt the Spirit of the Lord?"
Acts 5:8

Now when Simon saw that the Spirit was given through the laying on of the apostles' hands, he offered them money, saying, "Give me also this power, that any one on whom I lay hands may receive the Holy Spirit."
Acts 8:18-19

ONE IS TEMPTED TO DO EVIL when by some person or suggestion he is solicited to engage in the evil. Temptation may be a subtle or a bold suggestion, but it calls one to yield to a given course of action. Peter uses this word in the story of Acts 5, which we studied in the preceding chapter, with respect to a type of sin against the Holy Spirit. This sin is called tempting the Holy Spirit. It is man's attempt to get the Spirit to approve letting one have his own way. In Acts 8 we have an illustration of how this sin expressed itself in the life of Simon. As the story shows, tempting the Holy Spirit is asking Him to accept less than full surrender. It is something like the boy who prayed, "Lord, make me a good boy, but don't be in a hurry about it."

A moment's thought on the nature of Christian experience will reveal at once how serious this sin is. Man's basic sin is revolt against God. We are sinners, not so much for what we have done, but for what we are. Man is a sinner, not only because he has sinned, but because he likes sin! *The larger question in life is not what a man does, but why he does it.* Man's sin-nature is described in the words of the Bible: "We have turned every one to his own way" (Isa. 53:8). Within the heart of man there is only one throne, and it is occupied either by self or by the Spirit of Christ. The heart, meaning the seat of man's motivation, must be brought under the lordship of Christ. Only as man dies to the rule of self, and finds a new life under the reign of Christ, can he share in eternal life. Jesus said, "If any man would come after me, let him deny himself and take up his cross daily and follow me." (Luke 9:23).

An Example of Tempting the Spirit

The story in Acts 8 reveals the nature of this sin. Philip was being used of God in a great evangelistic outreach in Samaria. There was a tremendous spiritual awakening, and the city of Samaria was led to an understanding of the Messiah. Many believed and were baptized by Philip as an evidence of their faith in Christ. It is in this context that we discover Simon Magus, the magician.

"But there was a man named Simon who, had previously practiced magic in the city and amazed the nation of Samaria, saying that he himself was somebody great. They all gave heed to him, from the least to the greatest, saying, 'This man is that power of God which is called Great.' And they gave heed to him, because for a long time he had amazed them with his magic" (Acts 8:9-11). Simon, as a magician, had given the impression that he was some great prophet of God, using fake miracles to support his claim.

When Philip preached Christ in Samaria, light dispelled darkness and many believed in Christ. As they turned from darkness to light, they turned from Simon to Christ. Apparently, Simon decided it was to his advantage to join this movement, and we read, "Even Simon himself believed, and after being baptized he continued with Philip. And seeing signs and great miracles performed, he was amazed" (Acts 8:13). Later we discover the nature of Simon's belief.

There is a mental assent to the historical belief in Christ which does not save. The Bible says, "Even the demons believe—and shudder" (James 2:19). They know the truth of the gospel. Saving faith is more than mental assent; it involves a commitment of the heart to Christ. Paul outlines the way of salvation in Romans 10:9, "Because, if you confess with your lips that Jesus is Lord and believe in your heart that God raised him from the dead, you will be saved." Note, Paul does not say, "believe in your head," as though it is merely consent to some creedal statement, but "believe in your heart" that Christ is Lord. This heart-faith transforms one's life from the service of self to the service of Christ as Lord.

Just because Simon was baptized we do not conclude that he was born of God. In the following verses the evidence of the new birth is lacking. In like manner many people in Christendom today have been baptized into a church but have never been baptized into Christ! Many have only said yes to the instruction of catechism about Christ, but have never said an eternal yes to the Lord Himself. Unless one has committed himself to Jesus as Lord, he is yet outside of Christ and is not saved!

The next few verses reveal that Christ had not yet given the Samaritans the Holy Spirit. The church at Jerusalem, hearing of the faith in Samaria sent Peter and John as representatives of the believers to welcome into the fellowship these new converts. When these disciples arrived, they laid their hands on the new Christians and prayed for them, thereby identifying the Samaritan believers as a part of the one church of Christ, Upon this act, they were baptized with the Holy Spirit—a Samaritan Pentecost, accompanied by outward signs of confirmation. Why did the Samaritans need to wait to receive the Holy Ghost? The answer is found in the nature of Christ's lordship as Head of the church. In Jesus' discussion with the Samaritan woman in John 4, the woman mentioned the century-old conflict between worship at Mount Gerizim and the temple at Jerusalem. Jesus answered that the true church would center in neither, but in a spiritual relation with God. Thus in Acts 8, when the Samaritans believed, for the sake of the unity of the church, the Lord withheld the gift of the Holy Spirit from the Samaritans until the leaders of the Jewish church at Jerusalem were there to confirm it. This was God's way both of building the unity of the church, and transcending age-old animosities between Samaritans and Jews.

In our day of denominationalism, all Christians must remember that Christ is greater than any system! Although various denominations meet varied needs in the kingdom, they are valid only to the extent that they make Christ preeminent.

As Simon witnessed the laying on of the apostles' hands, and the evidence of the gift of the Holy Spirit, he made a strange request for a professed believer. The Bible says, "He offered them money, saying, 'Give me also this power, that anyone on whom I lay my hands may receive the Holy Spirit'" (Acts 8:18-19). It is obvious that Simon's life was still self-centered. He was interested in receiving divine power and privileges for personal advantage. Simon had not died to Simon! He had not given up the throne of his life to Christ. His was not a heart-cry for the presence of the Spirit in his own life, but for power to affect other lives. His self-centeredness was further revealed after Peter exposed his sin and pronounced judgment. He was not humbled to seek God's face, but simply asked Peter to pray for him "that nothing of what you have said may come upon me" (Acts 8:24).

Simon was still living for Simon, not for Christ. He was tempting the Spirit, or bargaining with the Spirit, to accept him on less than full consecration. Simon's sin prevented his salvation. Although the biblical story closes here, secular history reveals that the self-centered Simon became the first antichrist, of which John says, "now many antichrists have come" (1 John 2:18).

There is always the danger of playing with Christian truth rather than practicing it. One dare not deal carelessly with the truth of the gospel. A neutral position is impossible. One is either for or against, gathering or scattering. One is not an uncommitted person; rather, he is committed to Christ or to self. In the committed life there is always the imperative of loyalty. A man ninety percent faithful to his wife isn't faithful at all. Jesus said, "You cannot serve God and mammon" (Matt. 6:24). We will never have true revival until we break through the current shallowness and lay the foundation on bedrock.

Exposing the Sin of Tempting the Spirit

We do not know whether Philip had by this time discerned the evidence in Simon's life of lack faith or not, but we are shown that Peter was aware of Simon's hypocrisy. Filled with the Holy Spirit, Peter became conscious of the pretense in Simon's life. Note the words with which Peter exposes this sin: "Your heart is not right before God" (Acts 8:21). Peter goes right to the root of the problem, rather than dealing with the expressions. The expression in Simon's life was sinful, but there was a cause for that sin. The expression comes first, and is most obvious.

Simon's sin was expressed when he sought to purchase with money the spiritual powers displayed in Peter's life. Peter, immediately aware of the insult it is to God for man to feel he can purchase or earn God's grace, is most severe in his judgment. Peter's words expose Simon's true position, outside God's grace: "'You and your money,' said Peter sternly, 'may you come to a bad end, for thinking God's gift, is for sale?'" How often men tempt the Spirit, or bargain with the Spirit, to include them in God's gift of salvation, because of their gifts to the church, their deeds of charity, or their imitation of righteousness.

In exposing this sin, Peter cuts through the expression of sin to the cause. Of Simon, he says, "Your heart is not right before God.... You are in the gall of bitterness, and in the bond iniquity" (Acts 8:21, 23). Simon was jealous, because these men with their gospel of Christ had robbed him of prestige. Apparently he was jealous over the loyalty and praise given to Christ that heretofore had been given to him. Obviously his heart wasn't right before God, in that he had not surrendered to Him. Every man must deal with the problem of idolatry that would arise within his own soul.

The sin of tempting the Spirit is thus exposed as endeavoring to solicit the Spirit to accept less than full consecration. This is most searching. One tempts the Spirit when he asks for the Spirit's gifts in his life without surrendering to the Spirit's government! One tempts the Spirit in trying to dictate the terms upon which one will be a Christian. One tempts the Spirit when he asks the Spirit to approve and accept one's own way of life, rather than submit to the Lord's outline of discipleship.

One of the great needs of current Christianity is to rediscover the secret of the disciplined church. One of the benefits of the brotherhood of believers is that through the church the Spirit guides us in disciplining one another. The individualist is inclined to increase in egotism until he is useless to the larger cause. An egotist is only a zero with the edges rubbed off. In contrast, the brotherhood relation serves to create a well-balanced personality.

Many believers sin against the Spirit in opposing what He would do in their lives in spiritual discipline. They may react to the group and call it a hierarchy, but often go out and start a little hierarchy of their own! Such persons defend their present spiritual level and do not seek new heights. They sin against the Spirit in seeking to get His comfort without yielding to His control.

Emancipation from Tempting the Spirit

This sin is peculiar to those who, knowing about Christ, profess belief in Christ. The Christ-rejecting sinner out in the world is resisting the Spirit, but he is not bargaining with Him for salvation through "cheap grace." It is the person on the fringes of faith, one who does not wish to pay the price of commitment to Christ as Lord, who is guilty of this sin. Such a person would like to have one foot in the church and one in the world. He would like to have a "ticket to glory" without a transformation of life here, a Savior but not a Lord. Jesus is a person, not merely a provision, and you cannot dissect Him and take the part you choose, accepting His salvation without His lordship. Paul says that as enemies we were reconciled to God by the death of His Son, but "now that we are reconciled, [we shall] be saved by his life" (Rom. 5:10). Salvation comes through His lordship!

The deliverance from this sin is stated by Peter to be through repentance and faith. To Simon be said, "Repent ... of this wickedness of yours, and pray to the Lord that, if possible, the intent of your heart may he forgiven you" (Acts 8:22). To repent means to renounce, to turn from, to change one's mind, attitude, and behavior. The place where the change is needed is pinpointed by Peter as the "intent of your heart." The sin of tempting the Spirit is one in which the whole intent of the heart is opposed to the working of God's grace.

Peter said, God will forgive "if possible." Was Peter uncertain of the extent of God's forgiving grace, or was Peter emphasizing the seriousness of the sin? It must have been the latter, as Peter had been taught some personal lessons on forgiveness by Christ Himself. The "if possible" underscores the seriousness of the sin, for this sin is a deliberate shaping of the mind and conscience against the true working of God's grace. The danger is that persons may so condition their minds against the pattern of God's grace and around a pattern of their own conniving that they cannot come to share in His forgiveness. Forgiveness is free, but conditional. Man, living for self, is in revolt against God. God cannot justly forgive until man has brought that revolt to an end by turning to God in faith.

Sin is so binding that one may become wrapped up in self to the extent that he is hindered from turning to Christ. One might even have an imitation Christianity, but being self-directed, may never have committed himself to Christ, and thus would be outside God's forgiving grace. The most searching analysis of faith is to discern between a self-centered life imitating Christ and a life in which the self is surrendered to Christ. Self-righteousness is man's attempt within himself to achieve the approval and acceptance of God. This is the sin of tempting the Spirit, of soliciting His acceptance on a lesser ground than surrender. The only emancipation from this sin is absolute surrender of one's will to the will of Christ.

This message is very important for our time. Many persons who profess belief in Christ have never committed themselves to Him. Many are Christians only in name, like Simon. They may have been baptized into the church, but have never surrendered their lives to the lordship of Christ. Many churches offer a false assurance to those who give mental assent to the creed, but go on living a life of sin. Many carnal and worldly "Christians" are lost because they have not surrendered to Christ. They are guilty of the sin of tempting the Spirit, soliciting His approval on a type of Christianity never condoned by Christ. Paul states that, being saved by grace through faith, we are called to a life "prepared beforehand" that we should walk therein! (see Eph. 2:8-10).

We need a deep moving of revival in the churches of our time. Saints ought to begin praying for other church members as did Paul: "My little children, of whom I travail in birth again until Christ be formed [outwardly expressed], in you" (Gal. 4:19 KJV). Many who have made a profession of Christ have never known the presence of Christ in their lives. The spiritual deadness within churches is evidence of sinning against the Spirit, the life of the church. It is time we stop bargaining with Him to accept us with our sins and ask Him to save us from our sins. We must stop carrying over into the realm of so-called Christian experience those things which the Bible exposes as expressions of the flesh. Neither the church nor the individual will ever be spiritual when we seek to bring things from the kingdom of darkness into the kingdom of Christ and ask Him to sanctify and bless them. The Bible states, "That is why many of you are weak and ill, and some have died" (1 Cor. 11:30).

The call of the Spirit is that we confess Christ as Lord. The work of the Spirit is to make Christ Head of His church in a practical way. The church of the twentieth century needs to let Christ be Head, and honestly surrender to His lordship,

CHAPTER 8

Insulting the Spirit

*For if we sin deliberately after receiving the knowledge of
the truth, there no longer remains a sacrifice for sins, but a
fearful prospect of judgment, and a fury of fire which will
consume the adversaries. A man who has violated the law
of Moses dies without mercy at the testimony of two or
three witnesses. How much worse punishment do you think
will be deserved by the man who has spurned the Son of
God, and profaned the blood of the covenant by which he
was sanctified, and outraged the Spirit of grace?*
Hebrews 10:26-29

TRUTH IMPLIES RESPONSIBILITY, and for that reason many
persons do not want truth. Few persons in the world are willing to
take up the responsibility that truth demands. Many boast of knock-
ing at the door of truth, but if the door opened they would die of
fright. The Bible says, "Men loved darkness rather than light, because their deeds were evil" (John 3:19). Man's sinful heart prevents his being totally objective before truth, as his own heart has a
preference for evil.

When one turns his back on light, or better knowledge, he closes the door to moral and spiritual advance. Such a one seals his own
soul in the darkness of self-will. Life is a constant demonstration of
this fact. When one is open to the truth, he goes on with God in a

vital fellowship, while one rejecting the truth of God lives enslaved to the darkness which closed the door to truth. It is said that Stalin went to seminary and wrote on "Abiding in Christ," as found in John 15; that Mussolini was a theological student; that Khrushchev went to Sunday school as a boy and memorized much of the four Gospels! Atheism is not ignorance, but independence; it is a total rejection of God and an enthroning of self.

The great burden of the Epistle to the Hebrews is to expose the nature and seriousness of unbelief. Often the mistake is made of thinking of unbelief as ignorance of, or indifference toward truth. In reality, unbelief as used in Hebrews is "disbelief," a deliberate rejection of truth that has been perceived. The writer exposes the unbelief of Israel, in that after they had seen the miracle power of God, they didn't enter Canaan because of disbelief, the rejection of the power of God which they had earlier known. Disbelief knows that God has moved in the past, but will not commit the matter to God for today.

In contrast, belief is to trust everything to God. Belief is commitment to Christ not merely to a doctrine. In Romans 4 Paul shows that we are not saved by faith in our works of morality, nor by faith in observance of the Law, nor by faith in religious rites, but by faith in a Person. This faith enables one to live with a settled assurance in the promise and power of God.

The story is told that in Switzerland a valuable object was dropped into a crevice in the ice, too narrow for a grown man to enter. They asked a small boy if they could tie a rope around him and lower him to retrieve the object: The lad replied, "Yes, if my father holds the rope." Such is the challenge of faith in Christian experience, for it is God who makes good His own promise.

In Hebrews 10 the writer discusses our position in Christ as believers. A threefold statement of our sanctification in Christ appears early in this chapter. In verse 10, we are shown as having been sanctified positionally, by being in Christ (perfect tense in the Greek). Verse 14 talks of us being sanctified practically, as the Spirit of Christ witnesses within us (present tense in the Greek). And in Verses 16-25, he says we are sharing in a progressive sanctification in the fellowship of Christ.

It is in this context, of having magnified our saving and sanctifying relation in Christ, that the writer emphasizes the danger and seriousness of willful sin. This sin of which he speaks is not an occasional act of sin, but a willful, deliberate, continuous rejection of the truth one has known. The Greek present participle emphasizes the continuous nature of this sin. This sin is "apostasy from Christianity after having personally experienced its power and preciousness."[1] the word translated "knowledge" (*epignosis*) is not the word for intellectual perception alone, but rather the word for experiential participation! To receive and reject is the sin of insulting, of despising, of provoking the Spirit of grace (see Heb. 10:29). The writer uses this term of Israel's unbelief in chapter 3 as provoking God, calling those the days of "rebellion"!

The sin of apostasy, of turning from known and experienced truth, is one of the main themes of the Epistle to the Hebrews, The text of this chapter is the key passage, warning of the seriousness pf apostasy from the faith. While one is in such a state of rejection of truth as it is in Christ, it is impossible for Christ to serve as his advocate before the Father. Repentance is an attitude which is repudiated in apostasy. Faith is a fellowship which in apostasy is interrupted. God's grace is for sinners, but justly given only to sinners who repent, not to willful sinners who continue to revolt.

The Bible says, "Strive for ... the holiness without which no one will see the Lord" (Heb. 12:14). The believer is committed as in marriage and, rather than live in fear that the commitment will not last, should live in enjoyment of those aspects of fellowship that strengthen the union. In the Christian experience we are called to the same fellowship, and warned in the Epistle to the Hebrews to beware of apostasy or attitudes that lead to a spiritual "divorce." Of this, Robert Shank, in his scholarly treatise on conditional security, writes: "Apostasy, according, to the New Testament usage, constitutes defection, revolt, withdrawal, departure, and repudiation. An apostate, according to New Testament definition, is one who has severed union with Christ by withdrawing from an actual saving relationship with Him. Apostasy is impossible for men who have not entered into a saving relationship with God."[2]

The Choice of Unbelief

To understand why this sin is so serious and referred to as provoking God, and insulting the Spirit, we need to see the choice involved in unbelief. Willful sin, in its deliberate continuous nature, is a choice between Christ and the revolt of self. The seriousness of the choice is great; for when one chooses between fellowship with Christ and the pleasures of sin and prefers sin, the choice proves that he loves sin more than Christ! This becomes man's idolatry and condemnation. The Spirit of God has come to bring us to Christ and to magnify Christ in and through our lives. When one who has known the Lord turns again to "the weak and beggarly elemental spirits" (Gal. 4:9) of the world, it insults, provokes, and creates resentment on the part of the Spirit. In the third chapter of Hebrews the apostle's message is wrapped up in the words, "Take care brethren, lest there be in any of you an evil, unbelieving heart, leading you to fall away from the living God" (Heb. 3:12). Now with respect to the position of Christ, "as a son over his own house; whose house are we, if we hold fast the confidence and the rejoicing of the hope firm unto the end" (Heb. 3:6 KJV), the Spirit calls the believing heart to fidelity. The concluding verses of the chapter make clear the Spirit's call to a living, abiding faith in Christ. He warns against disbelief in the following words:

> For we share in Christ, if only we hold our first confidence firm to the end, while it is said, "Today, when you hear his voice, do not harden your hearts as in the rebellion."
>
> Who were they that heard and yet were rebellious? Was it not all those who left Egypt under the leadership of Motes? And to whom did he swear that they should never enter his rest, but to those who were disobedient?
>
> So we see that they were unable to enter because of unbelief (Heb. 3:14-16, 18-19).

The Occasion of Israel's unbelief to which the writer of the Hebrews refers is found in Numbers 14. When the twelve spies returned from an examination of the land promised to Israel, the people failed to claim God's promise and possess the land. Except for Moses' intercession, God would have destroyed Israel and raised up a new nation from Moses. God always rejects unbelief and unbelievers. However, through the prayer of a believing man, God listened to Moses and spared Israel. God exposes the issue in these words:

> "But truly, as I live, and as all the earth shall be filled with the glory of the Lord, none of the men who have seen my glory and my signs which I wrought in Egypt and in the wilderness, and yet have put me to the proof these ten times

and have not hearkened to my voice, shall see the land which I swore to give to their fathers; and none of those who despised me shall see it. But my servant Caleb, because he has a different spirit and has followed me fully, I will bring into the land into which he went, and his descendants shall possess it" (Num. 14:21-24).

Thus God presents unbelief as the willful rejection of the evidence of His presence and power at work. Israel, having seen God's glory and power, then turning aside, committed the sin that violated faith and robbed them of God's forgiving grace. As one footprint in the sand, in the story of Robinson Crusoe's island, challenged all the negative evidence and proved another's presence, so God's acts confronted Israel.

In his discussion of grieving the Spirit, René Pache shows the progression of sins against the Spirit, and writes of "doing despite to the Spirit of grace" (Heb. 10:29 KJV) as follows:

Despite to the Spirit of grace consists not of sinning and consequently grieving Him, whether once or on many occasions; for what believer is there who, through growing in spiritual stature, has not been made conscious of sins recently committed or until then unknown? In this passage, despite to the Spirit means willful sin by maintaining before Him an attitude of open revolt and by rejecting utterly the Son of God and the blood of the covenant.[3]

The writer of Hebrews in chapters 3, 6 and 10 points up the seriousness of knowing God and yet choosing the way of unbelief. In the passage under study (Hebrews 10:26-29), the Holy Spirit says that when one sins willfully, choosing unbelief rather than belief or commitment, "there no longer remains [no other or further) a sacrifice for sins, but a fearful prospect of judgment, and a fury of fire ..." (Heb. 10:26-27).

The Criticisms of Unbelief

Having looked at the choice of unbelief, we now examine further its nature. The nature of unbelief is exposed by its criticisms. As man's true character is revealed when he opens his mouth, in like manner the character of unbelief is revealed. In Hebrews 10:29 unbelief opens its mouth in criticism of the faith and thereby reveals its character. The picture is a black one, revealing the affinity of unbelief with the kingdom of darkness in its attack upon Christ. The serious nature of unbelief is emphasized in the words that follow in context: "For We know him who said, 'Vengeance is mine, I will repay.'" Add again, "The Lord will judge his people, it is a fearful thing to fall into the hands, of the living God" (Heb. 10:30-31).

This passage, similar in meaning to 6:4-9, reveals the hopelessness in apostasy from the faith for one who has had both knowledge and enjoyment of the provisions of the faith. The present participle in the Greek identifies the sin as a persistent rejection or apostasy. Thus, while one continues in that state, there is no way of coming to repentance (Heb. 6), and there is no other sacrifice for his sin than the Christ whom he is rejecting (Heb. 10:26). Thus, for one who has apostatized, there remains only the condemning judgment of God. The criticisms that unbelief expresses reveal the nature of apostasy.

1. Contempt toward the person of Christ. The writer says, "Who has spurned the Son of God ..." Apostasy (as well as false cults) is measured first by its attitude toward Christ. Unbelief tram-

ples underfoot the unique claims of Christ. The unbeliever is prepared to acknowledge Jesus as a great man, as a noble character and symbol of morality, as a great philosopher of religion and morals, and as a martyr to the cause of good in opposition to evil; but unbelief is inconsistent in claiming to acknowledge Jesus as a good (including honest) man and yet denying the unique claim of Sonship which He made.

The record says that Jesus claimed to be the Son of God, and that God substantiated His claim "by his resurrection from the dead" (Rom.1:4). One of the great laws of logic is that truth, to be truth, must be consistent. Jesus was either the Son of God or else He was not even a respectable man. The record presents Jesus as the Son of God! Unbelief renounces the claim of Jesus to be God's Son. Thereby the unbeliever sets himself up as the higher judge and authority and in his pride "has spurned the Son of God." The "disbeliever" thus places himself under the judgment and vengeance of God by the one deliberate act of rejecting Christ. In this act the unbeliever aligns himself with Satan in setting himself up against God. The unbeliever has placed more confidence in his own reason than in the revelation of God in Christ.

2. Contempt toward the atonement of Christ. The unbeliever has "profaned the blood of the covenant by which he was sanctified ..." an unholy thing. Apostasy from faith in Christ leads one to believe in his own goodness, and seek acceptance by God in his own merit rather than in the mediation of Calvary. The death of Christ is looked upon as a mere illustration that at times good must be ready to die rather than yield to evil, and thereby such a one is assured "true being" and is united with God. The expiatory values of the death of Christ are denied, since the blood of Christ is denied any propitiatory merit.

In contrast, the believer acknowledges Jesus as God in the flesh, paying the price of forgiveness at Calvary through absorbing man's hostility upon Himself. The cross stands as the evidence of both divine love and divine forgiveness. It is a valid forgiveness in that God Himself paid the price that justice demands for forgiveness: self-substitution. The blood of Christ never loses its power of meaning, in that Christ rose and lives with the eternal evidence that the price is paid for man's forgiveness by God (see Rom. 3:23-26).

Apostasy is rejection of the meaning of the cross, and the blood of Christ is despised. The blood is counted as "an unholy thing" (KJV), or as the death of a mere man, rather than the heart of the atonement. The unbeliever rejects the work of Christ, and may trust in the Law as a means of pleasing God, as though he may obey it well enough to be accepted. Yet, all men must confess that they have violated the Law and are thus condemned by their own standard. The Bible says that one who would live by the Law is obligated to keep it, yet no man has kept it. None have been saved by keeping it, and by it all are proved to be sinners (Rom. 4). The cross stands as the only place of forgiveness.

An illustration of this form of unbelief is revealed in a letter the writer received during a revival crusade in Salem, Oregon. A student of a liberal divinity school revealed his unbelief in his letter:

Gentlemen:

Despite the highly commendable objective of crusading for Christ, there yet remain some of us who have been overlooked in the general saving program. With this thought in mind, perhaps it would be to your best interests to contemplate the charming fact that not everyone who visits your tent revival has come to be born again.

As a disinterested bystander, I would highly recommend that you remove your rather expensive equipment to a place less openly tempting to the poor souls who've not had the benefit of accepting Christ's teachings as the personification of their super-egos. Realizing you place your faith in Christ, please don't make the unnecessary mistake of underestimating basic human nature.

May Christ be always with you,

Anonymous

_____ *Divinity School, '58*

Such is the downfall of many, who place confidence in the flesh, overestimating human nature, as though man has within him the potential to gain the approval of God, and thereby merit salvation apart from the blood of Christ and a spiritual birth.

3. Contempt toward the Spirit of Christ. One in a state of spiritual apostasy is also spoken of as having "done despite unto the Spirit of grace" (Heb. 10:29 KJV). The term "despite" means to go another way in spite of that which is outlined. The Greek word here translated "despite" is variously translated—to insult, to outrage, or to treat contemptuously. The unbeliever insults the Spirit of grace by following his own reason and rejects the Spirit's revelation. He treats the Spirit contemptuously when he relies on his own abilities to gain salvation rather than accept the Spirit's capabilities for his regeneration.

One insults the Spirit when, having been led by the Spirit to a knowledge of Christ, he deliberately rejects His power and asserts self in an attempt to be a "little Christ." The unbeliever outrages the Spirit when he rejects the divine presence, and claiming to have within him some spark of divinity, he trusts in his own so-called goodness, seeking to become another "little Jesus" by his own power.

The Spirit is here called "the Spirit of grace." God has both forgiving and enabling grace. The Spirit is active in bringing a man to share in God's forgiving grace; this is called justification before God. The Spirit is also active in sharing enabling grace, resulting in a transformed life; this is called sanctification before God. One cuts himself off from both the saving relation and the sanctifying relation with Christ when he is contemptuous of the Spirit of Christ.

The Condition of Unbelief

The condition of the soul who has insulted or outraged the Spirit of grace is spiritual estrangement. Such a one has cut himself off, by willful sin, from the only redemptive Agent the Godhead has in the world today. Reference was made earlier to Hebrews 3, where the effect of unbelief upon God is described as provoking God. It thus appears that the effect of unbelief upon the Spirit, when the apostate insults, outrages, and is contemptuous toward Him, is to provoke the Spirit. When the unbeliever insults and the Spirit is provoked or alienated, the result is spiritual estrangement. Since the new birth means new life, and that new life is a relation "in Christ," it follows that for the unbeliever to suffer spiritual estrangement is to have no saving relationship. This is no sudden estrangement but the result of a process of rebellion which caused deterioration.

The unbeliever is thus in a condition of being lost. To insult the Spirit is to cut one's self off from His saving grace. The Bible says,

''For by grace you have been saved through faith; and this is not your own doing—it is the gift of God'' (Eph. 2:8). The avenue of receiving grace, or the sphere of participation in grace, is ''in the Spirit.'' To sin against the Spirit of grace to the point of being contemptuous of His work, is to cut one's self off from the grace that brings about our salvation. Thus the condition of unbelief, of displacing Christ, aligns one with the Antichrist, both in attitude and in coming judgment

This sin is illustrated in the downfall of King Saul in the Old Testament. Saul was a man of spiritual privileges in his call, his praying friend, and in his spiritual experience. However, from Gilgal to Gilboa we discover his tendency to self-assertion. His weakness is revealed first in displacing God by substituting his opinions for God's oracles. We next discover that he is guilty of disobeying God, for he listened to the people rather than to God's prophet. Finally, we see that he departed from God, and as a result God departed from him (see 1 Sam. 15). He died a suicide rather than a saint. He wrote his own epitaph in his words to David, ''I have played the fool'' (1 Sam. 26:21). Just as Saul's sparing of Agag was a choice of earthly counsel over divine counsel, so unbelief places man's wishes ahead of God's will.

As a concluding observation, there is a sin found among many professing Christians who displace Christ by not counting Him sufficient for full salvation. Such persons think of grace primarily as forgiving grace and overlook enabling grace for the overcoming life, and seek to perfect their lives by the efforts of the flesh. To such people Paul writes, ''Are you so foolish? Having begun with the Spirit, are you now ending with the flesh?'' (Gal. 3:3). Such persons speak of faith and works, rather than of a faith that works, They separate the two, acknowledging a so-called saving faith and then adding works to it. In essence, they are saying that Jesus saves only part way, and we work out the rest. This is a sin of insulting the Spirit by an unbelief that does not recognize Christ as all-sufficient through His grace, and trusts in one's ability to please God. Such persons need to remember Paul's words, "For I know that nothing good dwells within me" (Romans 7:18).

Many unbelievers are such because of sin within their own lives, they do not want to believe and change their way of life. Others are unbelievers because of an intellectual pride that stumbles over the simplicity of the gospel and looks at the cross as foolishness. Some are caught in unbelief because they have failed to recognize the validity of faith in the promises of God.

A traveler through the northern part of the United States, in the early days came one cold day to the banks of the frozen Mississippi River. Afraid to trust the ice, he debated several hours until in the early evening he slowly started to inch his way across. Suddenly, in the dusk, he heard a man whistling merrily and looked up to see a farmer drive a team of horses and a wagon across the ice! Let timid souls look again to the lives of former pilgrims and to the proven promises of God as a challenge to their faith.

The answer to the problem of unbelief is belief. The answer to the problem of insulting the Spirit is to make Christ preeminent. The Spirit has come to glorify Christ. Only as the believer makes Christ preeminent in his life by belief or commitment to Him, is the Spirit both pleased and permitted to lead that person from one level of glory to another in the fellowship of Christ. Many careless Christians ought to repent by praying the prayer of William Cowper:

Oh, for a closer walk with God,
A calm and heav'nly frame!

A light to shine upon the road
That leads me to the Lamb.

The dearest idol I have known,
Whate'er that idol be,
Help me that idol to dethrone
And worship only Thee.

So shall my walk be close with God,
Calm and serene my frame;
So purer light shall mark the road
That leads me to the Lamb.

CHAPTER 9

Blaspheming the Spirit

Therefore l tell you, every sin and blasphemy will be forgiven men, but the blasphemy against the Spirit will not be forgiven. And whoever says a word against the Son of man will be forgiven; but whoever speaks against the Holy Spirit will not be forgiven, either in this age or in the age to come,

Either make the tree good and its fruit good; or make the tree bad, and its fruit bad; for the tree is known by its fruit. You brood of vipers! how can you speak good, when you are evil? For out of the abundance of heart the mouth speaks.

Matthew 12:31-34

TO BE IN OPPOSITION TO GOD is man's chief sin. There are various forms and expressions of sin, but the seriousness of the issue is in man's opposition to God. In the text under examination in this chapter, we face some of the most solemn words uttered by our compassionate Savior. The setting in which the words are found is significant, revealing that Jesus spoke concerning those who opposed His work, Jesus had come with the mission of revealing the Father, and in Him God revealed Himself. To oppose that revelation seals man in the darkness of human pride.

A wide variety of interpretations are proposed for this difficult passage. Many persons with a sensitive conscience have worried that they may have committed the unpardonable sin. G. Campbell Morgan often asked such persons what sin they felt they had committed, only to find they didn't know the character of the sin they worried about so deeply. It seems that those rebellious persons who may be involved in this sin never reveal concern. Many Christians who have sinned against the Spirit in ways mentioned in former chapters have experienced forgiveness, but still worry that they have "crossed the line." Satan uses ignorance of the nature of this sin to harass sensitive souls who know a limited amount about its nature.

A close examination of the passage in Matthew, with its parallel passages in Mark 3 and Luke 12, reveals clearly the nature of this sin, and its occurrence. This sin is called by Jesus "an eternal sin" (Mark 3:29), and everyone ought to understand its nature as well as its seriousness. The passage appears to indicate that the sin is more a condition than a single act.

Bible Teaching on Blaspheming the Spirit

The setting of this discussion reveals Jesus being rejected and ridiculed by the Pharisees. They blasphemed His name by attributing His power to an alliance with the prince of devils, Beelzebub. Some commentators immediately conclude, as does the Scofield Bible, that blasphemy against the Spirit is to attribute the works of the Spirit to Satan. Although this may be an expression of rejecting the Spirit and thus be a form of this sin, the passage would reveal something more searching. According to the context, these people were in reality blaspheming Christ, and in reply Jesus said, "Whoever says a word against the Son of man will be forgiven, (Matt. 12:32). Thus Jesus revealed that their rejection of His "human" person was not their most serious sin. They had closed their minds to what the Spirit wanted to reveal to them of Christ!

The Pharisees, not convinced of who Jesus was, might stand in opposition to Him as "Son of man," not understanding the identity of Christ in His earthy work and ministry, and yet come to forgiveness, However, to stand against Jesus out of ignorance of His identity was one matter, but to stand against what God was revealing through Christ by being closed to the Spirit of truth was another matter. The mind may be misled, and one may yet come to forgiveness; but when man's heart is set against God, there is no way to forgiveness. Ignorance is one problem, but not nearly so serious as being unwilling to be shown the way. In the Old Testament we read that the sin offering was for those who sinned "through ignorance," but not for those who sinned "presumptuously (see Num. 15:27-31.) The Pharisees were not only ignorant of God's work in Christ, but were closed to it, while Nicodemus, being ignorant of the full mission of Christ, was yet open to discover what God was doing through Christ.

The Scripture speaks repeatedly concerning the sin of being closed to the Holy Spirit who would lead man beyond precepts to a Person. God told Isaiah to take His message to a people so closed to truth and set against change that they would not believe lest they be converted. Four times this passage is quoted in the New Testament in description of persons closed to the truth as manifest in Christ! (see Isa. 6:10; Matt. 13:15; Mark 4:12; John 12:40; Acts 28:27). The meaning of these very difficult passages is explained by John in showing the contrast between Isaiah, who looked beyond the precepts and saw Christ, and those who, looking at the precepts, would not look to Christ. These persons were closed to the Spirit's work, lest they should hear, perceive, and become converted. Being satisfied as they were, they didn't want to change. Such are those today who avoid the gospel out of fear that they may be converted!

The sin of which Jesus was speaking was not of the mind but of the heart. It was not merely a mental attributing of the work of Christ to an alliance with Satan, but was a deeper matter of the heart being closed to what God was revealing to them in Christ. Standing against Jesus as a "man," as they understood Him, could be forgiven. But, for the sin of opposing what the Spirit of God wished to reveal through their conscience, there was no forgiveness. This is further emphasized in His direct words to them: "Either make the tree good, and its fruit good; or make the tree bad, and its fruit bad; for the tree is known by its fruit. You brood of vipers! how can you speak good when you are evil? For out of the abundance of the heart the mouth speaks" (Matt. 12:33-34). The sin is thus designated as an attitude of the heart that is closed to God's self-disclosure. This sin is eternal, and unpardonable in that such persons will never hear nor heed God's call of grace.

In interpreting the passage it should be noted that the opening words of Jesus are a promise of grace: "Every sin and blasphemy will be forgiven men." Here is a promise that places no limit on God's forgiving grace to cover deeds of sin, whether actions or words. However, there is no forgiveness for one who stands opposed to God's call, continuing his revolt against God. Such persons are described in the words of Jesus, "You refuse to come to me that you may have life" (John 5:40).

The Nature of Blaspheming the Spirit

How is this sin expressed in life experiences? In John's first epistle (5:16-17) he refers briefly to this sin as follows: "If any one sees his brother committing what is not a mortal sin, he will ask, and God will give him life for those whose sin is not mortal. There is sin which is mortal; I do not say that one is to pray for that. All wrongdoing is sin, but there is sin which is not mortal." Here John distinguishes between two types of sin—one not unto death and one unto death; the former pardonable and the latter unpardonable.

Sin does not primarily inhere in things, but in the attitude of the heart that wants the sin. Sin that is not unto death is apparently the type that comes through lack of victory or spiritual maturity, while sin unto death is the willful, presumptuous sin with an attitude of rejecting Christ. Sin unto death, turning from Christ in deliberate rejection, is to close one's soul to the work of His Spirit and thus cut one's self off from redemptive grace.

The sin of blasphemy against the Spirit, which sin never has forgiveness, is the final result of a person's persistent rejection of and disrespect for the call of the Spirit. The nature of this sin is in cutting off the revelation and redemption of Christ being testified to by the Spirit. One blasphemes the Spirit when he repudiates the Spirit's call to Christ as the one way of salvation This sin is due to man's basic sin of pride. It is eternal in its consequences, for when man rejects the work of the Spirit there is no other power to bring him to God. Man thus cuts himself off from God's only Agent of grace.

No person rejects truth without something happening within himself. One cannot turn his back on the light without increasing the darkness in his own soul. To reject the truth as it is in Christ is to remain a stranger to God, but it also is to become farther re-moved from ever knowing God. As one takes his stand against the Holy Spirit, he affects his own conscience. The conscience is given by God as a part of that image of Himself, which always calls man to what he understands is right. Even though cultures vary, and what is right varies between cultures, one factor is always consistent: the conscience always calls the mind to follow what is right.

The Holy Spirit uses the conscience as the avenue of conviction and call. When man rejects light and hardens his conscience, to that extent he has limited the ability of the Spirit to communicate with him! The Spirit may appeal on one point and, being rejected, may try another; however, each rejection closes avenues of His approach and increases the darkness and deadness within. Paul speaks of the conscience being "seared with a hot iron" (1 Tim. 4:2 KJV). It follows that after rejection of one approach upon another, a man's conscience may become so seared as to be "past feeling" and thus the Spirit can no longer get through to a man's heart with His convicting call.

Man is responsible for hardening his conscience, and by so doing closes the avenue by which the Spirit calls him. The sin of blasphemy against the Spirit is not some deed that a person commits causing God to cut him off in spite of his cries for forgiveness. This sin is of man's own choice and by it he places himself outside the realm of pardon.

In evangelistic work I once met an elderly man who said, "If I ever hear God call me again as He did when I was fifteen, I'll come!" I reminded him that he will never hear God call that clearly again and that he needs to respond by the spark of faith that is left. God may call just as loudly, but such a one has become hard-of-hearing spiritually.

The sin is unpardonable in that man who has so hardened his conscience by rejection of Christ that the channel by which the Spirit convicts is no longer open to His call. The sin is unpardonable because man, having so outrageously sinned against the Spirit, has severed himself from the only Power that could bring him to pardon. This does not mean that God would not like to pardon, for His love follows man to the very vestibule of hell. It is rather that man cuts himself off from the Spirit, the only person and power that can bring him to pardon. As Jesus said, "No one can come to me unless the Father ... draws him" (John 6:44). When man has severed himself from the drawing power of God, there is no way of coming to Jesus for pardon. This is the seriousness of eternal sin.

The Eternal Character of Blaspheming the Spirit

Jesus spoke of this sin as "eternal" in its nature. The New Testament speaks of man as immortal, having a beginning but never an end. Although the Old Testament suggests immortality, it isn't clearly shown; however, Paul says that Jesus has "brought life and immortality to light through the gospel" (2 Tim. 1:10). We believe through the revelation of Christ that man will exist forever. The believer will live with God as long as God lives! On the other hand, the unbeliever will live apart from God or be separated from God as long as God lives. The sin of persistent rejection of the Spirit's call is the expression of man's revolt against God; thus man writes his own sentence of being eternally separated from God. How long will man's hell exist? Hell endures as long as man exists—forever!

No matter how serious the sins a man may have committed, there is forgiveness with God. If man will respond to the Spirit's invitation, God will forgive. The thing that keeps man from the forgiveness is not the size of the sins but the self-will or *size* of the man. Paul referred to himself as the chief of sinners, yet God forgave. Paul goes so far as to say that God saved him, great sinner though he was, as a guarantee that if God could save Paul, He can save all who come after him. Paul expresses this truth in the words, "But I received mercy for this reason, that in me, as the foremost,

Jesus Christ might display his perfect patience for an example to those who were to believe in him for eternal life" (1 Tim. 1:18).

It also follows that the character of this sin makes it eternal. This sin is deliberate rejection of truth brought to bear upon one's conscience and soul. Jesus said in our text that all other sins can be forgiven. With God our attitude is more important than our acts. One desiring to serve God is accepted even though his service is imperfect. On the other hand, when one's attitude is against God, he is condemned by his attitude rather than by his acts. Paul speaks of his own black past and depth of sin and adds, "But I received mercy because I had acted ignorantly in unbelief" (1 Tim. 1:13). Thus there is a sinful behavior of an "unbelief through ignorance" for which there is mercy, but in unbelief of the known truth (discussed in the previous chapter) there is no pardon. Paul adds in several of his testimonies that he had "lived before God in all good conscience up to this day," meaning that he had lived in harmony with his understanding of God. This honesty before light, as he received it, is the reason God was able to give Paul a further, unusually brilliant, revelation and also account for his transformation in such a decisive and obedient way. It's thrilling to realize that God can and will forgive the deepest of sin where one is open to His call. However, when one closes himself to the call of the Spirit, he seals himself in the isolation of damnation.

Having thought on this passage, we are faced again with the decision for or against God. All sins which a person may commit can be forgiven by God except heart-opposition. In the final judgment man's destiny is determined by the state of his heart. The people of whom Jesus spoke were religious in practice, but they were not redeemed persons. Their hearts had not been given to God, but remained under the control of self.

Blaspheming the Spirit

If I gained the world, but lost the Saviour,
Were my life worth living for a day?
Could my yearning heart find rest and comfort
In the things that soon must pass away?

If I gained the world, but lost the Saviour,
Would my gain be worth the lifelong strife?
Are all earthly pleasures worth comparing
For a moment with a Christ-filled life?

Had I wealth and love in fullest measure,
And a name revered both far and near,
Yet no hope beyond, no harbor waiting,
Where my storm-tossed vessel I could steer.

If I gained the world, but lost the Saviour,
Who endured the cross and died for me,
Could then all the world afford a refuge
Whither in my anguish I might flee?

Oh, what emptiness without the Saviour
'Mid the sins and sorrows here below!
And eternity, how dark without Him!
Only night and tears and endless woe!

What, though I might live without the Saviour,
When come to die, how would it be?
Oh, to face the valley's gloom without Him!
And without Him all eternity!

— Anna Olander

CHAPTER 10

Displacing the Spirit

But when Cephas came to Antioch I opposed him to his face, because he stood condemned. For before certain men came from James, he ate with the Gentiles; but when they came he drew back and separated himself, fearing the circumcision party.

Galatians 2:11-12

GREAT HEIGHTS ARE NEVER REACHED without disciplined behavior. Discipline is both costly and demanding. Success in any area of life is achieved by the disciplines that lead to it. The businessman succeeds in proportion to the disciplines of management, The physician succeeds in respect to the disciplines of medicine. Education is gained in a given field through the disciplines of that program of study. The minister succeeds in proportion to the way he gives himself to the disciplines of prayer, Bible study, and the leading of the Spirit. So, in all of Christian experience, we succeed in proportion to the way we accept the disciplines of the Spirit of Christ.

One of the sins within the church is that of displacing the Spirit who would lead the church. We push the Spirit aside for something else and rob Him of his rightful position. The first responsibility of the church is to ascertain the mind of Christ through the insight brought by the Spirit. We displace the Spirit when we give more attention to the will man than to the mind of Christ. It is the Spirit's work to conform believers to the image of Christ (see Gal. 4:19), and this can never be accomplished unless believers humbly honor His leading. We are not only concerned about the new birth, but about the newborn; not only about a decision, but about discipleship!

On a number of occasions in the New Testament individuals or groups failed to honor the Holy Spirit. One of them, selected as a background for this discussion, concerns Peter and his behavior in the church at Antioch (see Gal. 2:11-12). By examination of this incident we may learn something of the tendency on the part of men to displace the Holy Spirit.

Displacing the Spirit in the New Testament

In Galatians 2, Paul reveals an incident which happened in the church at Antioch. Peter had come from Jerusalem to visit the young church at Antioch. The church at Antioch was interracial, made up of Gentiles and Jews, white and black. Not being a Jewish church, it was nicknamed with the descriptive title, "Christian" (Christ-followers). "In Antioch the disciples were for the first time called Christians" (Acts 11:26). Peter had learned, by the vision received in Joppa and by the gift of the Holy Spirit to the household of Cornelius, that God accepts believing Gentiles on the same basis as believing Jews. Peter had defended his fellowship with the household of Cornelius before the Jerusalem Church by the argument that God had given them the Holy Spirit also (see Acts 11:17). Now, in the account in Galatians, Peter visits the church at Antioch, demonstrating this new insight by eating with the Gentile Christians. By so doing, Peter proves his understanding that God accepts them and so will he. This is the testimony needed to safeguard the unity of the church.

However, Paul reveals that during Peter's visit some of the Jewish believers from Jerusalem came up to Antioch, and for fear of them Peter "drew back and separated himself." The account says he did this "fearing the circumcision party." This act caused those Jews who were circumcised to form a separate party, thereby bringing division into the church at Antioch. The tension was so severe that even Barnabas was caught up in it and aligned himself with those requiring circumcision. Peter was motivated more by the ultraconservatives from Jerusalem than by the leading of the Spirit of Jesus. When Paul took note of this partiality and offense to the unity of the Spirit, he said, "I opposed him to his face, because he stood condemned" (Gal. 2:11).

Examining this sin we would first of all accuse Peter of being *two-faced*, which he was. It appears that we need a reminder that even after having received the Holy Spirit in such a marvelous way as Peter had, he still was not a perfect man. Sanctification does not bestow infallibility on anyone. The sin-tendency remaining in him should have been counteracted by the Holy Spirit. We might also lay at Peter's feet the charge of partiality, remembering that concerning it James says, "This wisdom is not such as comes down from above, but is earthly, unspiritual, devilish" (James 3:15). Both of these sins are deplorable. However, something even more serious was involved.

Peter had told Ananias that in lying to the church he was really lying to the Holy Spirit. He needed now to be reminded that in his own attitude at Antioch he was sinning against the unifying work of the Spirit. The fact that Peter had dealt with Ananias, prayed for the Samaritans, and had seen Cornelius baptized with the Spirit, increased the seriousness of his sin. Just as Jesus asked Paul when he was persecuting the church, "Why do you persecute me?" (Acts 9:4), so here Paul reminds Peter that sin against the church is really sin against Christ! In view of the seriousness of Peter's offense, it was not surprising that the Holy Spirit raised up Paul as a voice, and as a lesson to the entire church group. Paul "opposed him to his face ... before them all" (Gal. 2:11, 14).

One of the great values of the brotherhood of disciples is the balance of discipline. What Peter was inclined to justify in his own life was justly exposed by Paul. Our concern as believers should be first to examine ourselves rather than to judge others, lest we mistake their motive. However, occasions of disunity which lead to division need to be corrected by the Spirit's guidance. In this instance, Peter was guilty of displacing the Spirit, and so the Spirit used Paul to discipline Peter.

Displacing the Spirit in the Church Today

Peter's sin of being a respecter of persons is not absent from the church today. Far too often men are more concerned about pleasing their fellowmen than they are about the approval of God. There are occasions, as at Antioch, when men may hide their intolerance behind good biblical terms and seek to force others in the church to follow their wishes. Such persons not only disregard Romans 14 but sin against the great spiritual principles of love, equality, and unity among the brotherhood. Rather than forming cliques of persons who agree and cut the church fellowship into groups, each individual should submit to spiritual discipline for his own life and thereby be exemplary to others.

A personal relationship with Christ does not exclude discipline, but rather begins with it. No satisfying intimate relationship is possible between persons apart from the necessary disciplines that create and confirm that relationship. In Christian experience, no person can profess Christ as Lord without the first disciplinary step of renouncing the lordship of self. Thus giving up of self and enthronement of Christ lies at the heart of a satisfying, sanctifying Christian experience. This behavior is not forced upon a person, but springs from an inner motivation of the Spirit. We displace the Spirit when we ignore what He is doing through the group. We also displace the Spirit when we trust in group pressure, group dynamics, or group disciplines to do what God intends for the Spirit to do by inner conviction.

When a group forces discipline upon a person rather than demonstrating it to him, it usually results in a reaction rather than a response. The church has done the best job of disciplining when it has taught the individual how to mind the Spirit and thereby to discipline his own life. We displace the Spirit when we seek to manipulate people rather than aid the Spirit in bringing them to spiritual insight.

We displace the Spirit when we are satisfied with a church that is "in order" with certain regulations which involve *things*, but is not conformed to the image of Christ. In Galatians 4:19 Paul expresses concern for such church members in the prayer "Christ be formed in you." In this phrase he the Greek word *morpho*—here translated meaning "outwardly expressed." The real purpose of the Spirit's work in the church is to lead every believer "to mature manhood, to the measure of the stature of the fullness of Christ" (Eph. 4:13). Any church that does not live with this heart-cry is not a New Testament church, but as Paul says, is a follower of "another gospel" than that of Christ. The church that lives with this concern as the very beat of its pulse will find continual life and growth.

We displace the Spirit when we seek to perfect believers by legislation rather than by spiritual life. Obviously, many persons have never stepped from the threshold of introduction to Christianity into the experience of identification with Christ. Some so-called Christians live by the question, "Can I do such and such and still be Christian?" This is as intelligent as arguing how close one can drive to the precipice and not go over. Such a person is more in love with self than with Christ. Our interest is in seeing how close we can walk with Christ.

Independence and intolerance reveal that those, who have these traits have never taken the death route, dying to the old nature so that they may live for Christ. To appeal to their self-motivation to conform to the group for acceptance has not changed their selfish hearts. They need to be led to yield to the Spirit until their desire is, "How can I better express Christ?" Only by placing the Spirit at the center of the church and at the center of the individual's life can we develop true spirituality. Only by the Spirit's work can we answer our problems of carnality and worldliness, sensuality and secularism, criticisms and contentions, indifference and intolerance, lukewarmness and legalism, intellectual sophistication and individual snobbishness.

We displace the Spirit when we pass our own judgment upon worldly practices and approve them because they are the accepted thing in our time. Even though we have the message of the Spirit on principles of holiness, love, separation, and service, we wish to sanctify some worldly things for our pleasure. The Spirit is displaced when, boasting a so-called liberty in Christ, one prides himself in being progressive enough to adapt Christianity to the modern mind.

Man's nature is still the same, and the redemptive mission of the Spirit is to transform man's life by the gospel. True being is found in a simple faith relation with Christ, rather than a philosophical approach to an impersonal God. The Spirit tells us, "Do not be conformed to this world but be transformed by the renewal of your mind" (Rom. 12:2).

Ministers need to beware of going with the crowd rather than speaking up op crucial issues. Peter should have spoken as a voice for God, but he was cautiously looking out for his own good. Many men have failed to mind the Spirit when they could have stood in the gap and prevented some deadening trend. For some, the Bible teaching on holiness is too unpopular in a church that has become worldly, and to save themselves they are silent. For others, patriotic feelings may cause them to be silent when standing for truth would be unpopular and praying for their enemies unacceptable.

Again, Paul's appeal for a nonconformed life adds to the tension between the believer and the unbeliever; therefore, rather than risk a "scandal" among men, it is ignored. However, Jesus said, "He who does not take his cross and follow me is not worthy of me. He who loses his life for my sake will find it" (Matt. 10:38-39).

Overcoming This Sin Against the Spirit

Paul takes his stand in the Galatian episode, not on the authority of mere human opinions, nor of human traditions, nor of a system of religion, but on the authority of Christ as divine revelation. For Paul, Christ was "bigger" than any system or creed. Creeds grew out of man's experience with Christ, and we need to let the creed point us back to a meaningful experience. Paul thus answers the problem of displacing the Spirit by testifying to the centrality of Christ. By placing Christ above all that points to Him, the Law and religious rites, Paul corrects the problem which caused the division at Antioch. As a personal testimony, Paul said, "I have been crucified with Christ; it is no longer I who live, but Christ who lives in me; and the life I now live in the flesh I live by faith in the Son of God, who loved me and gave himself for me. I do not nullify the grace of God; for if justification were through the Law, then Christ died to no purpose" (Gal. 2:20-21).

The Spirit of God is given back His place in the church when the church lives in search of the "mind of Christ." To organize, legislate, and pass actions in accordance with what is most advantageous to our mind-set rather than consciously to seek the mind of the Spirit is sin. Once again the church must take seriously the challenge of prayer and study of the Word until it can be said, "It has seemed good to the Holy Spirit and to us" (Acts 15:28).

The Spirit of God is given back His place when we trust Him to work within lives of new believers. Why do many Christian workers and church leaders think they must do all the work? Why should we pressure people into a certain way of life rather than respect the wooing of the Spirit? Is not God's pattern conviction rather than coercion? If the churches of our day would give more time to edification than to entreaty, more to practice than to pressure, and more to testimony than to a tirade of admonitions, persons might he more readily convinced of the values of faith. To overdo the sales talk and underemphasize the satisfaction of soul may often prevent success. We need to trust more in the presence and power of the Spirit and less in the pressures of the flesh.

The church of the twentieth century is weak and worldly. We need a return to New Testament spirituality that will go beyond anything we see today in the professing church. We will not get this by bigger and better church buildings. We need better church members. We will not answer this need by merely educating the percentage of our members who go to college. The entire brotherhood needs deeper spiritual insight. It will not be accomplished by better organization, although that is often needed, but by strong dynamic motivation. It will not be achieved by a simple, easy passing of regulations to be enforced, but by an introduction of spiritual realities to be enjoyed. Ours is the challenge of placing the Spirit at the heart of His church. By making Christ preeminent the church will actually become a dwelling place of God through the Spirit.

Come, Holy Spirit, come!
Let Thy bright beams arise;
Dispel all sorrow from our minds,
All darkness from our eyes.

Revive our drooping faith,
Our doubts and fears remove,
And kindle in our breasts the flame
Of never-dying love.

Convince us of our sin;
Then lead to Jesus' blood,
And to our wond'ring view reveal
The mercies of our God.

Dwell, therefore, in our hearts;
Our minds from bondage free;
Then shall we know, and praise, and love,
The Father, Son, and Thee.

— Joseph Hart

CHAPTER 11

Honoring the Spirit

Not by might, nor by power, but by my Spirit, says the Lord of hosts.

Zechariah 4:6

EVERY GENERATION faces the challenge of building the church of Christ in its own time. God's program is to take out of the world a people for His name. He is doing this by building a church which becomes the visible presentation of the work of God in the world today. Christ works through the church to demonstrate the dynamic, transforming power of the gospel.

Mankind is caught up in tension and turmoil the world over. The perpetual struggle for supremacy divides the nations of the earth. There is a revolution of the masses coupled with the struggle and tension between the races. The cold war causes man to shiver at the antagonism between communistic nations and what is known as the free world. The problem of inequality continues between those who bask in the luxury of plenty and those who are always in want. We need stability in a society that has become so self-centered that it would practically destroy itself. Individuals violate moral principles in efforts to attain their own desires. The problem of fear and frustration burdens the hearts of those who have not found the broader dimensions of life in which man partakes of eternity. Underlying all of this there is the basic problem of man's sinful heart which pits the wishes of self against the Word of Christ.

In this kind of world God is using believers to build the church. The task seems almost impossible, and yet God's Word comes with His answer: "Not by might, nor by power, but by my Spirit, says the Lord of hosts" (Zech. 4:6). A task may appear impossible, but by faith it soon appears attainable, and then it is done! This Word from the Lord undergirds the believer's faith. Zechariah was a prophet to the remnant which returned to Palestine after seventy years of captivity. God had commissioned Zerubbabel to rebuild the temple of Jehovah. The task appeared impossible, for there was limited manpower and lack of an army to safeguard the workers from enemies.

In this moment of discouragement God sent a message to Zerubbabel, saying, "Not by might nor by power, but by my Spirit, says the Lord of hosts." God added that not only had Zerubbabel laid the foundation of this house, but his hands would also finish it. Even though the beginning appeared to be small and weak, God asked, "Who hath despised the day of small things?" (Zech. 4:10 KJV). The word would be achieved by God's own means and methods. This text produces a vision of faith. The relevance of this text is to discover how these words became a promise to the leader of Israel. On the same grounds, this text becomes a promise to all who build the church of God in our time.

A Promise to Those Doing Cod's Work

The building of the temple was by commission of Jehovah Himself. The Christian worker must be certain that the program to which he has given himself is of the Lord. There is always the danger of a man asserting his own interests rather than following the direction of the Spirit. A person may be misled and become a follower of some fanatical ideas which turn him away from the true program which God has outlined. It has been said that "a fanatic is one who runs faster when he sees that he is on the wrong road." On the other side, there is danger of becoming so satisfied with the status quo that God cannot lead one into ventures of faith.

As a Christian, one ought to be thrilled to share in the body of Christ and be anxious to express his Christianity in the group of his fellowship. Many Christians are too apologetic for their own church and its position. If we are certain that we are in a program approved by God, we should proceed accordingly. One need never apologize for those aspects of his faith which are expressed out of love for the Lord Jesus Christ. Ours is a challenge of being loyal witnesses and workers in the fellowship where we are called.

In knowing that what one is doing is of the Lord, we need to understand our relation to the larger thrust of God's redemptive program. When one becomes an individualistic Christian and shuts himself off from the larger church, he robs both himself and the total witness of Christ of the benefits which mutual sharing provides. As members of a particular group, our attitude toward others dare not be one which excludes, but rather challenges in the fellowship of Christ. One's commitment is made to Christ, and sharing in the fellowship of the church becomes the opportunity to enrich one another through the convictions the Spirit of God has created. No church is made up of perfect people, but we can have the evidence that the church is made up of dedicated people. The ground of fellowship is the certainty that one is "in Christ," a blood-washed, redeemed person.

A spiritual church is one that has discovered the meaning of brotherhood in Christ. When one is saved, he does not stand alone but is a part of the larger body. Paul writes of the church that we are all members one of another. Again we are told to "bear one another's burdens, and so fulfill the law of Christ" (Gal. 6:2).

The impact of our lives upon each other is one of spiritual challenge, on the one hand, to discover the meaning of love as it bears patiently with differences in personality and thought, and, on the other hand, to be positive in the encouragement of spiritual insight and growth. As a glowing coal removed from the fire and laid on the hearth soon loses its warmth, so a believer severed from fellowship with others suffers lack. Paul writes to the Corinthians concerning a brother who sins and thus is disciplined by God and a spiritual church, that those who are spiritual are to surround him with love in the hope that he may be brought to confession. The believer must share the compassion of Christ for all men.

A work that is of God must be consistent with the primary purpose of the church in the world. That purpose is evangelism, calling persons from the way of sin to the way of Christ. The place where worldliness is hitting the modern church most is not on the front line of evangelism, but in the home churches that have become lukewarm and indifferent.

One of the greatest means of combating worldliness and complacency is for the homes of our churches to rediscover the challenge of evangelistic witness. When each family shares in prayer concern for neighbors who are caught up in the spirit of the world, they accomplish two things. First, in their own family they sharpen the consciousness of the difference between one committed to the way of Christ and one given to the way of the world. Second, they develop within their family a sense of redemptive mission which will safeguard them as they move about in the world. The problem of worldliness is never defeated by withdrawal but rather by witness.

The church grows in proportion to the degree its adherents are committed to witness. However, a soul-winning congregation is not motivated by legislature but by love. God does not merely command soul-winners, He creates them. As compassion comes with awareness of need, a passion for evangelism is not generated by organization but by association. The vision of the field does more than the schedule in the file or the map in the foyer. Some pastors, confronted with a lagging program, may feel like the sales foreman of a business concern. The foreman and plant manager were conferring over a map upon which numerous pins marked the activities of their salesmen. Contemplating their low returns the foreman remarked, "Perhaps it would do more good to take the pins out of the map and stick them in the salesmen."

A Promise to Those Discerning the Spirit

In the New Testament the Spirit of God worked to make the gospel dynamic in each individual situation. On the day of Pentecost the Spirit of God reached 3,000 souls as the believers, numbering at least 500, brought friends and neighbors to hear the gospel through the ministry of the Apostle Peter. On other occasions, as in the case of Philip on the road from Jerusalem to Gaza, one lone person was confronted with the gospel and brought to Christ.

Under the ministry of Paul, there were occasions when a whole city was turned upside down in a spiritual revival, burning books and breaking idols, as persons by the hundreds yielded themselves to the call of the Spirit. On the other hand, there were occasions when the Apostle Paul was used of the Spirit to lead a single individual to the Lord.

In discerning how the Spirit works, we discover in the New Testament outreach principles of operation which must be realized today. In contrast to physical power, the Spirit moves by truth and love. His evangel is one of conviction and compassion. God does not force persons to become Christians; neither can Christian workers press individuals into the body of Christ. The Spirit of Cod wins souls to Christ by communicating Calvary love. We need to learn from the Holy Spirit what it means to love those around us who are neither a part of our group, our background of thought, nor our way of life. A growing church is always breaking down sociological barriers to create a spiritual brotherhood.

In contrast to manipulating people, the Spirit works by inner conviction. The Christian worker is challenged to discern how the Spirit of God is working within the life of the person to whom he is witnessing. Helping a person to peace with Christ we need to discover the stage of development in his march of faith, A convert's progress must not be by coercion but by instruction. One's witness may not see the full step of faith, but can serve as one step forward. To force a person beyond his comprehension and true commitment is to sin against the nature of faith.

Every person has certain psychological hungers, of wanting to be accepted, approved, and appreciated. We need to beware that persons may respond to a church group and adopt its standards from a mere psychological hunger rather than because of concern for holiness. Persons may conform to find acceptance and approval in a given setting rather than commit themselves to the person of Christ out of inner conviction. True acceptance on the part of the Christian worker means accepting a man for what he is, and in this acceptance discovering ways of enhancing his insight and experience.

In contrast to static forms, the Spirit of God makes revelation dynamic. The Word becomes spirit and life again as the Holy Spirit selects that truth which is needed at the moment. Our challenge is to discover by His guidance what God is saying to this particular need. The ability to make the gospel relevant today is not something which comes by human insight, but rather by divine unction. We need always to pray for the gift of the prophet in the church, not in the sense of foretelling but of *forthtelling*. God's truth will speak to any time and culture, but only as the Spirit guides in its application.

In contrast to having an "in-group," the Holy Spirit gives acceptance to all who come to Him. It is much easier to fellowship freely with those who are part of our own type of thought than to broaden our thinking and understand those about us. We often fail to win souls by simply excluding them from our fellowship. It might help us to reflect on how tolerant God must be to accept the varied thought patterns in a given congregation. With those variations God still grants to each heart a sense of His acceptance and love. In our modern society we must learn from the Spirit how to communicate a sense of divine acceptance to those estranged from God. Winning the lost is not by might, nor by power, but by His Spirit.

A Promise to Those Yielding to the Spirit

There is much insistence that the coming of the Holy Spirit is a group experience rather than an individual experience. There is valid reason for the emphasis upon the group experience, as a corrective for those individuals whose claim to have received the Holy Spirit leads them into the sin of self-centeredness. The egotist is one who concludes that he is the all-important person, even in God's program. Such a one is like the woodpecker who was pecking on an oak tree which was struck by lightning. When the oak tree split, the woodpecker died, thinking he had done it! Although we need this group emphasis as a corrective, we dare not forget that there is an individual experience with the Holy Spirit. God deals with the individual in salvation and also in the reception of the Holy Spirit. Individualism and collectivism must be brought together to share fully in the work of the Spirit.

The promise of this text must become personal just as salvation is personal. For the individual there must not only be a doctrine of the Holy Spirit but a dynamic birth of the Spirit. In Christian experience there must not only be a baptism into the church but a baptism with the Holy Spirit. Each individual Christian must come under the control of the Holy Spirit. One must be taken over by the Spirit of Christ.

For the Spirit-filled Christian, discipleship is not only a matter of following Christ but of fellowship in the Spirit of Christ. There is always the danger of an imitation discipleship which is purely the human effort of following the example of Christ. This individual yieldedness to the Spirit makes possible a life of Spirit-possession.

Every Christian must meet at least five conditions to share the promise of this text. There must first be that humility which hungers for a greater work of grace. Second, there must be a consecration that surrenders everything to Jesus Christ. Third, there must be definite prayer to be filled with the Holy Spirit. Fourth, there must be an exercise of faith which appropriates the power of the Spirit. Fifth, there must be an honest commitment to obedience. The Scripture says, "For sin will have no dominion over you, since you are not under law but under grace.... But now that you have been set free from sin and have become slaves of God, the return you get is sanctification and its end, eternal life" (Rom. 6:14, 22).

A decade ago, A. W. Tozer gave a chapel talk at King's College on "The Deeper Life." With acknowledgment to Dr. Tozer, his points are used here to clarify the way to spiritual power.

1. Vow never to be dishonest about sin in your life. We must always reckon with the gap between the Creator and the creature and live in an attitude of repentance.

2. Vow never to defend yourself. We seem to have been born with our fists clenched. Self-defense prevents the Spirit's transforming ministry.

3. Vow never to own anything. A good steward may hold title to property, but he holds it as under God. David Livingstone said, ''All that I have I hold in relation to the kingdom of Christ.''

4. Vow never to pass on anything hurtful about others. A lot off malicious gossip parades in the form of prayer requests. Paul said, "Who art thou that judges another man's servant? To his own master he standeth or falleth.

5. Vow never to take any glory to yourself. God can bless the man with whom He has found His glory is safe. God will not give His glory to another, lest it interfere with the redemptive mission of the Gospel,

The church of our time faces the tremendous challenge of building the kingdom of Christ. We are living in a day of exploding population. Every week, there are one million more souls in this world who need to know Christ. We need a church that is virile and victorious, definite and dynamic, transforming and triumphant.

A dying church is one that cannot save its own. A static church is one that saves its own. But a living church is one which adds to its fellowship persons who are won by evangelistic outreach beyond the borders of its own families. Our challenge is to share in the kind of faith that produces such a living church in our generation. By God's grace it shall be done, not by might, nor by power, but by His Holy Spirit.

Endnotes

Chapter 1/The Transforming Spirit
1. Paul M. Miller, *Group Dynamics in Evangelism* (Herald Press, 1958), 143.
2. Bryan Green, *The Practice of Evangelism* (Scribner's, 1951), 21.
3. Romans 10:9, free translation.
4. For a fuller treatment of this distinction regarding the baptism with the Holy Spirit, see Merrill F. Unger.
5. For an excellent treatment of perseverance, discussing the question of conditional vs. unconditional security, see *Life in the Son* by Robert Shank (Westcott, 1960).
6. G. Campbell Morgan, *The Spirit of God* (Revell, 1953), 23.

Chapter 2/The Sanctifying Spirit
1. Brunner, *The Divine Imperative*, 53.
2. Chester K. Lehman, *The Holy Spirit and the Holy Life* (Herald Press, 1959), 39.

Chapter 5/Grieving the Spirit
1. René Pache, *The Person and Work of the Holy Spirit* (Moody Press, 1954), 139f.
2. Ibid., 109.

Chapter 7/Tempting the Spirit
1. Acts 8:20 from *The New English Bible*. © The Delegates of the Oxford University Press and The Syndics of the Cambridge University Press, 1961. Used by permission.

Chapter 8/Insulting the Spirit
1. *Pulpit Commentary*, 284.
2. Robert Shank, *Life in the Son* (Westcott, 1960), 158.
3. René Pache, 110.